Michele Hanson was born in London and grew up in Ruislip. Her first short story was published in 1977. Her first column, about local government, began in 1983 in the *Guardian*. It was followed by *Treasure*, which will appear as an animated cartoon in Spring 2001. Her current *Guardian* column, *Age of Dissent*, has been adapted for radio. She lives in North London with her mother, daughter, partner and Boxer dog. The combined ages of the members of this household add up to 232 years.

Also by Michele Hanson
TREASURE
WHAT TREASURE DID NEXT

The Age of Dissent

Collected from her *Guardian* columns

Michele Hanson

A *Virago* Book

First published by Virago Press 2000

Copyright © Michele Hanson 2000

The moral right of the author has been asserted

A CIP catalogue record for this book
is available from the British Library.

ISBN 1 86049 825 6

Typeset in Goudy by M Rules
Printed and bound in Great Britain by Clays Ltd, St Ives plc

Virago Press
A Division of
Little, Brown and Company (UK)
Brettenham House
Lancaster Place
London WC2E 7EN

This book refers to no real characters, living or dead, especially not Jennifer, Tanya, Carol, Hazel, Nova, Clare, Ian, Martin, Syrrel, John, Dicky, Jimmy, Val, Olga, Jacqueline, Shirley, Elisa, Esther, Nicholas, Nina, Myland, Alison, Anne, Munch, Christine, Ronald, Richie, Hilary, Ginny, Finny, my daughter Amy and my mother Clarice without whom . . .

Contents

Michele Hanson

Michele Hanson

The Age of
Dissent

Beginning of the End

It's a difficult age, fifty-three. Birthdays whiz by, the body deteriorates. No wonder people feel glum. I notice that the bottom of my thigh is beginning, very slightly, to hang over my knee. This is surely the beginning of the end. I don't think I shall fight it. I have been advised to drink lots of milk and do weight-bearing exercises.

'What are they Doctor?'

'Walking.' I do this daily with the dog so I'm all right. I shall conceal the overhang with clothing, or not care. It's that or a total body support stocking and mask. All around my peers are busily having face-lifts. I have a stare at Mrs X at a party. She has had one. She certainly looks very smart, her face lovely and smooth, all those spider naevi gone, the cross-patch lines stretched out, and she has cleverly positioned herself with her big fat bottom in the corner and the lovely new face glowing out at everyone, so no one notices the bottom.

She had the face done in America, says she, where they know what they're doing. And oh look! There's Mrs Y. She's had one too. I look closely. No visible signs. No stitch marks, no frill of skin round the side where it's all been gathered up and tied in a knot. Or was it the lip-fattening that she had?

My friend Gillian has had a bosom implant. She, for a change, wants to look older, like a mature woman. She's never had a bosom in her life, even after three children, just two small flaps on her chest. Even the doctor sympathised and granted her new bosoms on the National Health. She is thrilled to bits with them. They look perfect and stick out like anything, almost pneumatic and slightly rude-looking. She now lives happily with her three children and new bosoms in the country. Her husband visits at weekends.

I have heard that such bosoms go lumpy if you go out in the cold. I warned Gillian to wrap up warmly. And do they deteriorate like ordinary bosoms? Will the face-lifts droop back into creases and the new fat lips shrivel again? I hear that one often has to have the face relifted two or three times. Perhaps people should just walk on their hands or stand on their heads. Then the skin would drop the other way, smoothing out the wrinkles, without all that painful surgery, danger and expense.

'Oh who's that lovely woman standing upside-down,' people would call out. 'Her complexion is perfect.'

And being upside-down is of tremendous benefit to haemorrhoids. As the body falls apart, the piles tend to fall out rather more. They too need to be pushed the other way.

'What shall I do for the best Doctor?' I have asked. 'Lie down, sit down?'

'Try standing on your head,' said the Doctor. It was her little joke, but perhaps more sensible than she knew.

But physical deterioration can be put to good effect. My Grandma, an astute businesswoman, slightly fiddled the prices on the garments in her shop during the war. She charged a little more that she should have done and didn't pay her purchase tax properly. Then she was found out and had to go to court.

She pulled her grey hair into wild, sticking-out strands, put her hat on wrong and took her teeth out.

'I'm a poor old woman,' she whimpered at the jury. 'My husband's run away and left me with three children and the shop to look after (which was true) and I don't know what I'm doing.'

The jurors' hearts melted, Grandma got off scot-free and built up a flourishing business in the High Street. Not that I condone Grandma's fraud, but she did have a more positive attitude to ageing. And luckily for her no one ever saw your knees in those days.

Escape from Death Row

I have just rescued my mother from Wessex General Hospital, or the antechamber to Hell.

'Don't send her there,' I begged the Doctor, the Sister, the Nurses and a Manager. 'Her husband recently died there on a trolley, her sister-in-law developed huge and fatal bed-sores. She'll think she's never coming out again.'

They sent her there.

'We have a bed crisis,' Sister rings me apologetically at ten at night from the Wessex County. 'We're sending her to Wessex General.'

'We call it Death Row,' I drone.

'Oh I wish you wouldn't,' says Sister prettily. 'It's not that bad.'

My mother has angina. She is very anxious, say all medical staff. The anxiety is making the angina worse. Then they send her to Death Row to relax.

I whiz down from London to get her out. It is unpleasant having an elderly parent incarcerated in such a place. She is wild to escape, dressed and striding up and down the ward waving her stick, the only patient moving. The others are very pale and mostly asleep. The odd subdued visitor sits in attendance. It is deathly quiet. But we cannot leave. My mother's supply of pills is missing. Pharmacy cannot find them. This is obviously another ploy to minimise anxiety. Another delay. Just as we are about to leave in a bate without them and return later, the pills appear. We escape at last and whiz to the post office, the fish shop, lunch club and hairdresser. No angina. My mother rings the doctor to report her release.

'What do you want now?' snaps the receptionist. I am keen to dart round and give her a sharp slap but my mother is used to this. She is eighty-nine and has seen it all before.

'I have gout, fits and pains in my chest,' my father told his doctor not so long ago.

'You are eighty-three,' said the Doctor in a grump. 'I'll be lucky if I live that long.' He zoomed in and out in a trice and hurried off to the next patient, and there are hundreds along the South Coast, all suffering from Eighty-three, or even Seventy-three, and all the ages in between. Ill health can be a grey area for the elderly. After a certain age in Sussex and along much of the South Coast and in other parts of Britain, one cannot be ill. Only old.

I think there may be a useful catch here for the Health Service. If one is Eighty-three rather than ill, then it's Social Services' responsibility rather than Health Service. Health Service is free, but Social Services has to be paid for by the client. The Health Service can make enormous savings on people who are found to be Seventy, -Eighty-three.

My father was taken into hospital after a fit and lay in bed babbling temporarily.

'What's he like at home?' the nurses asked us in a concerned way. 'What's his quality of life?'

'Perfectly all right,' we said. 'He visits the betting shop daily, reads the runners, selects winners, goes to Waitrose, drives the car, reads about World War Two in depth.'

'We shan't resuscitate if he arrests again,' said the nursing staff gravely. 'Quality of life,' they murmured. 'What's he normally like?' they asked again. 'We take his age and record into account.'

'He's perfectly all right,' we shouted, 'There's nothing wrong with his quality of life,' but they didn't believe us. And then they consigned him to Death Row, with a skeleton staff of angelic, overworked, underpaid nurses to look after the glut of geriatrics. But perhaps Management felt there was no point in their doing very much. The patients were after all suffering from Eighty-three, a hopeless condition with no known cure. My father escaped twice, confounded them, recovered his speech and his quality of life. The third time finished him off. Thank goodness we escaped. For now.

If You See Me Walking
down the Street

A quiet, modestly dressed and well-behaved grey-haired woman is often unnoticeable. People have been moaning about it recently, but it has its advantages. Rosemary and I noticed it on our brief holiday in the Canary Islands. We were not offered time-share properties. This was something of a blessing, but rather odd. Why not? We looked fairly affluent. We are both professionals with passable careers. We could have afforded one. Meanwhile, all around, on the beach and in the bars and restaurants, salespersons were out and about begging everyone to buy time-shares except for us.

Sometimes the salespersons came up so close that we could even hear them plotting away, how to swindle the next punter, rehearsing their lines, as if next to ghosts, because women with grey hair do not count.

No one even noticed our swimwear. This was another stroke of luck. The new style bikini, cut high at the sides, does not look fetching now that my bottom has more or less collapsed.

All in all, seaside holidays become more relaxing as the years whiz by. We were able to sunbathe, swim and eat out in a leisurely way without being pestered and with no one bothering to jeer at our beachwear.

I can't say that I mind being ignored in the street or on holiday. I spent a very unpleasant day in Naples in my youth, unable to pause for one second to gaze into a shop window without a loathsome bottom-pincher looming up behind me. And I had carefully put on my dreariest garments – a dull, loosely fitting T-shirt and baggy jeans, hoping for a quiet outing. I went with a chum in a brown floral and asexual frock, her hair in short plain brown curls, but we might as well have been two pieces of raw meat in the lions' den. We had to give up our tour of Naples, return to the boat and hide in a darkened cabin.

Back home the nuisance continued. 'It's Olive Oyl,' roared the men on building sites as I passed by, tall and thin with a pin head. Olive Oyl was not as highly regarded then as she is now.

Much better to be old and dull and wander the streets in peace. Then you have a choice. And you can always command attention if necessary. My mother does it. She merely shouts and waves her stick. Waiters, salespersons and members of the public jump to it at once. I have learnt, when in need of attention, to follow her example: dress in bold colours, dye the hair, speak in a loud and piercing tone, rap the ground or surrounding furniture with a stick or umbrella, and people will take notice in a trice. If there is one thing the public cannot bear to see it is a woman, age forty-five-plus, behaving badly or noticeably in public. It embarrasses them enormously. They will do anything they can to stop it.

Olga over the road is still noticed without even trying. As she is an artist, her outfits are rather more striking than Rosemary's, and chaps whistle as she whizzes by on her bike, shorts on, bum in the air. 'I'm still moderately fit from a distance,' says she modestly – from all that bike-riding, swimming and striding about the Himalayas in her holidays. 'Thank goodness they can't see my face,' she thought to herself in a moment of weakness the other day, then pulled herself together and considered turning back and giving them an aftershock and telling-off. It was, after all, the wrong sort of attention.

And yesterday a pleasant young man offered me a seat on the tube. How kind. I am now obviously seen as an exhausted old bat. At fifty-three. But I was longing to sit down. I am not averse to being noticed occasionally.

Hove Is Where the Heart Is

My mother is in turmoil. She must make a horrid decision and she can't. Shall she move in here with us or shall she stay in her own lovely flat in Hove? There, things are all on one level. She has two lavatories, one bidet, comfortable chairs, peace and quiet and tidiness. But she cannot spend the nights alone. All sorts of dreadful things may happen: angina, heart attacks, robbers, vertigo, nightmares, insomnia, loneliness or sudden death. These are the things she lies sweating and expecting when she sleeps alone.

But in our house she is safe. I am on hand to summon the doctor or ambulance. Unfortunately, our home is dreadful. It is full of mountainous stairs, mess, dribbling barking dog, noise, rows and screaming daughter and granddaughter.

And the sofa is too low, the chairs too narrow, the stairs too many and too steep, the meals too late, the tea too weak, the whole place too messy and the gardener and visitors irritating.

It's only a pretend choice anyway. She doesn't really have one, which throws her into a fury. She must come and live here with us in Hell. It is at least entertaining. She tries to be positive about it. And we have better services up here in town: the doctors, the dentist, the hospital and the social workers are charming. Down in Hove they tend to be curt, surly and always in a hurry, perhaps because of the glut of elderly people down there. And the social club up here is superior. There is bridge, dancing, bargain hairdressing, and the lunches are divine. Her friend there, Esther, asks her a difficult question over lunch.

'Tell me Clarice,' she says, looking rather anxious, 'you're living with your daughter. What's it like? Because I might have to do it.'

'I told her,' says my mother, tactful as ever, 'that you do things your way and I mustn't interfere. That's the way you run your life.'

This must be an edited version. But what will Esther do? What will several million other Aged Ps do but leave their homes and live with their children, or watch their life's savings evaporate in a trice paying for residential care.

A drear thought. We cannot bear my mother to do it. She does not want to end up sitting in a dull semi-circle of brown or green armchairs watching the telly. At least most people in our house can walk about. If we all try to scream less, put in a downstairs lavatory, train the dog not to dribble and bark, make nice strong tea and early dinners, things would improve no end.

Meanwhile, my friend Rosemary's mother is rather envious of my mother. She longs to move into her daughter's home. But Rosemary has the poorly husband to look after, and three children and a cat and a full-time gruelling job. This is not an easy time of life. Rosemary and I are beginning to long for retirement, when we will be able to sit about reading large biographies. I shall send my mother over on Sunday to give Rosemary's mother the lowdown on life with a daughter, her adolescent child, dog, paramour and messy house. It will be a realistic picture. My mother is not one for toning things down. She tends to speak frankly. She has herself considered sheltered accommodation, but even for that one has to pay through the nose.

'I might as well be miserable here,' says my mother sensibly.

Bad Hair Days

My friend Olga is having a slight hair crisis. Being an artist she has never been one for convention, but now, at fifty, she feels that some sort of style change is in order. She has felt this for months. Meanwhile her hair has looked quite wild and begun to disturb my mother. She cannot understand Olga's delay or crisis. To her the solution is simple – a cut, rinse and set is in order.

'Why doesn't she do something with her hair,' my mother moans persistently. 'It looks terrible.' She has asked Olga this same question repeatedly, but Olga does nothing. She is para lysed by indecision and as time goes on her fringe grows longer and my mother becomes more agitated. Olga's visits to our house are nerve-racking. Will my mother say something untoward?

Forgetting that her critic is in residence, Olga rashly calls round for coffee. I have warned my mother strictly not to comment, but the thought of Olga's hair has tormented her all week. She knows that women of our age may not walk about looking unkempt. For months she has racked her brains for a solution and now she has found one. She is bursting to speak.

'I've been worrying about you for days,' she says to Olga, 'and today I had a good idea.'

'What is it?'

'Well, I know you don't like spending time on your hair, so why don't you buy a wig? You can get some lovely ones.' She is thrilled with her solution. Olga laughs bravely. I reprimand my mother. She is unrepentant. 'Next to *her*,' she says ruthlessly when Olga is gone, '*you* look glamorous.'

We have a yawning generation gap here which opened in my youth in the Sixties and will never close. My hairstyle and mode of dress have always rather disappointed my mother and Olga's is far more outlandish. And she is bolder than me. Even now, on the downhill slope to death, she still refuses to tone it down.

But I shall always think fondly of Olga's hairstyle – it is similar to mine – thin, weedy, uncontrollable and bound to distress a neatly coifed mother. I remember it at a depressing ante natal lecture that Olga and I attended in earlier middle age. I arrived first. All around sat neatly dressed couples and I sat alone with my hair in a mess. Then suddenly in burst Olga in a cloud of pottery dust with her hair in chaos. At last an ally for me in this hell-hole.

'I want you to make friends with your vagina,' said the lady speaker in a forthright way.

Olga and I weren't sure that we wanted to do that. We both left the lecture quick as a flash and jumped onto a bus screaming – two elderly prima gravidas without proper hairstyles. But now sixteen years have gone by, our children have grown up and we must get ourselves in order. Our hair is now almost universally disapproved of. People will not tolerate it. Luckily for her, Olga's child is a boy, but mine is a girl who longs for a chic mother. I do my best, have my hair cut regularly, dye it reddish-purple, apply mousse after washing to give it body. People smile politely at it.

Olga and I did recently find one admirer, however. We were at a party with another witch-like friend with an outrageous pink coiffure. We had made an effort, put on our best frocks, but our hair still lacked control. A strange, bald young man in a black cloak approached us. He was full of admiration.

'It's wonderful to see women of your age with character,' he said. It almost sent us all off for a neat cut and set.

Sex Later On

My friend and neighbour Rosemary is desperate for her own bedroom. She has found sex something of an ordeal in recent years. After twenty-five years of marriage, she would far rather join a choir, but she has her husband to consider. He would not prefer the choir. He tends to sulk horribly. So Rosemary has struggled on. She would map out Sainsbury's on the ceiling, starting in the fruit and veg area, then through dairy products and all round, and by the time she got to soft drinks and the checkout, she'd have a trolley full and it would all be over. Husband never knew about the map.

But this week she's had enough. 'I've told him,' says she, 'that that part of our life together is over.' Rosemary looks thrilled. The husband is monosyllabic but Rosemary is determined to stick with it. She feels that at our age, a choir is more fitting. And she has her mother and children to look after, as well as the sulking husband. She needs to do something pleasant with her spare time, spiritual rather than physical. At her age, fifty-six, she has rather given up on sex. It seems to be a slightly ridiculous and troublesome pastime which luckily fades out in later middle age.

But not for all of us. My mother has just spent a week down in her seaside home with a friend, tidying and throwing out rubbish. While tidying they chatted about this and that and up came the topic of sex. My mother is eighty-nine and has rather forgotten about this topic, but her friend hasn't.

In fact she is tremendously keen on it and has a boyfriend. At seventy-nine. My mother returns with a startling report. Not only does her friend have a sex life and speaks of it rather boldly, but she also told my mother that recently it had not been up to the desired standard. She was not having orgasms.

'She has a boyfriend,' says my mother, shocked to the core, 'and she wants orgasms as well?'

The friend has had the effrontery to go to the doctor and complain. She wants things put right. The orgasms are a must. Luckily some medicament that she was taking had been causing the problem. It was changed and the thrilling sex life resumed.

I tell my mother that nowadays women may go to the doctor and ask such things. If they dare. I must say I rather admire this lady. Demanding such rights at her age, or at any age, is a courageous step, even hidden away in the doctor's surgery. To tell a relatively new friend or any acquaintance, when one is elderly and on the chubby side, is even bolder.

Being rather staggered by her friend's revelations, my mother didn't like to ask too many questions, but she did manage one. 'Doesn't he mind all this?' she asked, pointing to the friend's pudgiest area.

'He loves it,' said the friend, in a carefree way. This must be a liberated woman – sexually uninhibited, no weight problems. For thirty years my mother has battled against excess fat, and here is a woman, far chubbier than her, who couldn't give a fig. How has she done it?

At art school, when I was only seventeen, we had a rather swizzy painting teacher, possibly in his fifties, who tried to broaden our education a little by introducing some literature and a dash of his own philosophy. He read out D. H. Lawrence in dialect (an embarrassing experience for us), and told us that sex was an Art and improved with practice. Naturally we thought him a dreadful show-off. But perhaps he was spot-on.

My mother's friend is having the time of her life. Heaven knows what might happen to Rosemary in the choir.

Elderly Residents

My mother is now here to stay. She has the bedroom on the first floor next to the bathroom. So has Angela's mother over the road and so has Rosemary's husband next door. In our street it is the most suitable room, nearest to the bathroom so that people can stagger there in a trice.

We now have three generations in our house. This makes for a volcanic combination: the elderly mother, the menopausal daughter and the teenage granddaughter doing GCSEs. We are battling illness, hormones, terror, exams and death. Naturally there is tension in the home.

Rosemary and I used to share childminding to give each other a bit of time off. Now that the children have grown up, more or less, we are minding my mother and Rosemary's elderly husband. This is tremendously handy, especially if, like Rosemary next door, one is trying to hold down a gruelling job and the husband at home won't cook a crumb for himself but *will* stagger out for cigarettes and fall over.

He often does it. Last time the kind newsagent brought him home in a car. He did it when Rosemary was out on a thrilling weekend course. It seems to happen when Rosemary is out enjoying herself or holidaying rather than working. She tries a relaxing walk with me and the dog but is burdened by guilt.

'What if he's slumped dead over the table when I get back?' But he isn't. He is safe at home, chain-smoking in an airless room glued to a giant Wordsworth biography.

Michele Hanson

It is difficult for Rosemary to be high-spirited. 'How can I go away?' says she, after the newsagent episode. The words 'day centre', 'stroke rehabilitation' and 'counsellor' revolt the husband. Rosemary has searched endlessly for a club for very clever, insolent, uncooperative and chain-smoking stroke victims but cannot find one. She is forced to leave him unattended.

'Go,' we all shout. 'Have a break. We'll check.' I will supervise dinners. Off she goes for a weekend in the country. Straight away the husband disappears. The oldest daughter rings up in a flap.

'Dad went to the library at eleven o'clock and now it's five o'clock and he isn't back yet.' We rush out in the car and search the route to the library. Will he be lying on the pavement in a pool of library books, mistaken for a drunkard and ignored by passers-by? Has he been knocked down while bumbling across the road? No. There he is slumped on a bench in the boiling sun in his winter jacket and weighed down by biographies.

'Where have you been Dad?' ask the children, wiping their eyes and blowing their noses.

'Stopped for a beer and a sandwich,' says he defiantly and staggers back to the armchair for another death-defying smoke.

During the week I go out for dinner leaving my mother at home alone. Social Worker tells me I must have a social life. It's Rosemary's turn to be minder. She promises to supervise my mother's dinner and bedtime, but when she goes round to check, my mother is in a dreadful state. The angina has been raging and she is planning her funeral. This is tough on Rosemary after a gruelling day as a bereavement counsellor. Hopefully her skills will not be necessary.

Luckily they are not, and the funeral plans can be cancelled. But we do call the doctor and my mother is whizzed off to the Whittington for a check-up. It is a four-star palace compared to her own Death Row hospital down by the seaside. She is given a cup of tea almost at once, doctors swarm around, lunch is served in A and E and dinner immediately she reaches the ward. In Death Row one can wait eight hours for a drop of liquid or morsel of food. She is keen to move into the Whittington immediately and permanently.

But she recovers and must leave. 'Marvellous,' she says to the porter. 'People should pay to stay here.'

Porter's jaw drops open. 'People don't often say things like that to us.'

But not everyone has recently escaped Death Row and come to live in our house.

How to Behave

There is an unwritten code of conduct for the elderly. They must dress neatly and modestly and behave with decorum. Loud voices, immoderate laughter and outlandish clothes are not acceptable. Nor are wild and impassioned or uninhibited gestures. Everything is to be calm, quiet and demure. Outrageous behaviour is the preserve of youth. In anyone over fifty it is seen as problematic. Bold decoration of the home is permissible and may even be regarded as charmingly eccentric, provided one sits calmly in the middle of it.

Our home is now a mélange of my mother's Hove baroque rococo and my stripped pine, rampaging spider plants and spatterings of the Sixties. American visitors admire it tremendously.

'It's *charming*,' says the distant cousin over from New York.

'Bloody shithole,' mumbles my mother rather coarsely, but that is one thing the elderly are allowed to do – speak their mind. She does not sit quietly among the eccentricities of her surroundings.

Unfortunately she and I both have loud voices and my dog is rather large and messy. Young persons naturally tend to shy away from us and the teenage daughter is often mortified. And now Rosemary next door tells me that my hair still looks rather unkempt.

It won't do. One must beware of long, loose hair in later years. It only looks like the mad woman up in Jane Eyre's attic, says Rosemary strictly. It was all right for her, locked away up there out of the public gaze, but when one is out and about, people will only laugh and point at long, wildly flowing grey hair. I shall have it neatly cut and have a dark rinse.

I had considered buying another dog, to keep mine company, but it is perhaps sensible to have only one dog or cat. A woman of fifty-plus seen about with streaming hair, gumboots and three dogs is presumed mad. So is a man, but less so.

And I have taken to lying on application forms. At fifty one should really step down obligingly and make way for youth and new ideas: the Internet, cultural materialism, market forces. An employer rarely welcomes an applicant of fifty, or even forty. Much better to have a young fellow of twenty-five recently down from university, less set in his ways, computer-literate, arteries clear, decades away from death and decay and unlikely to be ravaged by male menopause. And cheaper.

And it is rude to have sex after forty-nine. It may offend younger persons. The thought of it makes them shudder. It is perhaps a little easier for them if their original parents are still there as a unit. Then the children may assume that nothing happens any more. How could it? The parents must surely be bored with it by now. And things seize up. Function is impaired. Provided the parents maintain absolute silence once in their bedroom, then the young may relax.

But if the withered parent finds a new partner, the children are naturally distressed. They know something horrible may be going on which could be visually unacceptable.

'You're disgusting,' screams my daughter. 'You're always doing it. Yuk.' She is wrong of course, but I cannot convince her.

The daughter or son may be at their most beautiful, nearly adult, fresh, flawless, no wrinkles, no varicose veins. It seems to them that the unattractive may not enter paradise. We, the elderly, must choose more moderate pursuits: gardening, tapestry, walking the dog, reading quietly. No drink, drugs, sex or rock and roll. I think I am allowed to study.

Dangerous Encounters

My mother is tremendously forthright. 'I didn't know you had such fat legs,' she roars cheerily at Olga, who is wearing some new boldly-patterned leggings. She doesn't really mean fat, she means not skinny, but this doesn't help Olga. She laughs bravely, although knocked sideways by this harsh critique.

I remind my mother that such personal remarks are hurtful, but she is unashamed. 'I like fat legs,' says she. 'John Cleese has got lovely legs.' She has admired them ever since *A Fish Called Wanda*. To my mother, plump is beautiful. She stares tragically at her elegant twiglike teenage granddaughter, remembering the chubby cuddly baby that she once was. 'You used to be such a lovely fat baby,' she moans in public. Granddaughter is mortified.

We live on a knife-edge. People are being offended right, left and centre. An outing with my mother is even more fraught with danger. She will attack members of the public physically and verbally. The size, strength and ferocity of the victim means nothing to her. Only yesterday she chose a huge bare-chested fellow with bulging, rippling muscles and a bullet head for a telling-off.

This gentleman was strolling across the road with his three small children as we drove up it to a T-junction at a slow crawl. He flew into a fury, as if we had roared past shaving the skin off his nose and within a whisker of slaughtering his children.

'Arsehole,' he bellowed.

24

Naturally my mother was horrified. 'That's no way to speak in front of children,' she roared, 'You're the arsehole.'

If she had thought for one nano-second before speaking she would have realised that it is foolish to correct and speak abusively to a fellow of his stature when one is eighty-nine and when he is only two feet from your wide-open car window.

He approached the window in a menacing way, growling vile threats at my mother, who argued back fiercely. I ordered her to remain silent but she refused. She rarely obeys orders, especially from her own child. Luckily a gap appeared in the traffic in the nick of time and we whizzed to safety.

'Please don't do that again,' I warned my mother. 'Do not shout at men like that. He doesn't care that you're a frail old lady. He nearly punched your head in.'

'He wouldn't dare,' she snapped boldly. 'I'd have hit him with my stick.'

What luck that we managed to escape. My mother has not realised that the Nineties have been a fairly brutal period when being eighty-nine and female never saved anyone from a punch on the nose. In fact muggers find frail old ladies rather tempting. They can steal purses from them effortlessly. One half-hearted slap and the old ladies go down like ninepins. I have warned her never to open the door when I am out and never to walk about the streets carrying her handbag.

Minutes later she realised the error of her ways. 'I should think before I open my mouth,' she said sensibly, shaking with terror at the thought of what might have happened. She only expresses such sentiments *after* a burst of kamikaze behaviour.

In this instance right was on her side. This fellow deserved a drubbing. Had I only been six foot six, male and muscular, I too would have given him a telling-off, but even after eighty-nine years on this earth my mother has not learnt that one is not necessarily rewarded for being right. She has, however, realised that the meek shall inherit nothing at all. It is becoming more and more difficult to sort out one's morals.

Brain Rot

My dog is going grey – a horrid reminder of its mortality. It only has two or three years to go. That means that in the next few years I shall lose my dog and my mother and my daughter will probably leave home. Meanwhile I am constantly going to funerals. These have a cumulative effect. Every new funeral reminds me of all the other funerals and that my turn is looming.

Things are worse for my mother. She makes a new chum at her club, talks to him for a few weeks and then suddenly he isn't there anymore. Dare she make any more new chums? I notice that the club has a Keep Fit class. I point it out to my mother as she queues up to book her dinner.

'Why don't you join the Keep Fit?'

'Yes,' says the woman behind the counter. 'You should try it. It's very good for you.'

My mother is outraged. 'I'm not doing that,' bellows my eighty-nine-year-old mother. 'They're a load of old geriatrics.'

The woman next to her is the queue glares rather crabbily.

'That's very rude,' I say. I feel obliged to reprimand my mother. She couldn't care less. She thinks the elderly look unattractive in leotards and shorts and refuses to join in, but eventually realises that she has perhaps been slightly offensive.

'I'm a geriatric too,' she shouts, laughing fiercely, and stamps off to make new friends, if she dares. It is obviously terrifying being eighty-nine with death glaring you in the face. No wonder she gets bad-tempered.

And now I have had a cone biopsy. Is it cancer? Threatened by death, I am suddenly keen as mustard to live till ninety, even though it is an increasingly nerve-racking business.

The doctor is reassuring. It is not cancer. I may live for years and years, physically, but what about the mind? I am a little worried about it. I forget things – like what I've just walked into the kitchen for. I stand thinking, I gaze about. I retrace my steps. The mind has gone blank.

Walking healthily on the Heath the other day with Sylvia and our dogs, I thought of a strikingly interesting thing to say. I waited politely for Sylvia to finish her sentence without butting in, which was a mistake. By the end of her sentence, I'd forgotten mine.

'Rack your brain,' said Sylvia.

'There's nothing there.' The very interesting thought never came back. I found this rather depressing. And I am having difficulties with the shopping. Only yesterday I forgot to buy vital cooking oil and lemons. My mother had begged me repeatedly to remember these items. She even wrote me a list, but I forgot it. Even if I had remembered the list, odds on I would have forgotten to look at it. Naturally my mother is exasperated. She is the one meant to be wandering about in a daze.

But I am apparently worrying needlessly. The mind does not necessarily degenerate. It can, with practice and exercise, even improve. It just changes method. Its knowledge becomes crystallised rather than fluid, so I hear. It may be less flexible than it was in my youth, but it has by now built up an enormous wodge of information which, mixed with experience, becomes wisdom. People should be rushing round here for advice. I could be a village elder keeping the culture alive. In China my wrinkles would be greeted with admiration and joy. What a pity that I live in North London, where they are viewed with distaste.

27

At least one can combat short-term memory loss, so a pamphlet tells me. You must visualise your thoughts. If you're going out to buy sausages, visualise yourself as a personalised sausage, perhaps pushing the shopping trolley. That should do the trick.

Will I remember to do that?

Travels with Mother

Rosemary and I walk the dog across the Heath. It is stunningly pleasant, the sun shining, lakes glimmering, leaves changing colour and trees looking ravishing. I think my mother could do with an uplifting outing like this, gliding along the paths in a comfy wheelchair. I shall hire one for a try-out, plan the route carefully and avoid steep hills and mud patches.

Upon my return home, glowing from the charming walk, I tell my mother this plan. It throws her into a grump.

'I'm not sitting in a bloody wheelchair,' she shouts ungratefully. 'I can walk.'

But she can only walk a few yards. She cannot reach the more attractive areas of the Heath. Rosemary's mother would kill to be pushed about in a wheelchair and pandered to. If she heard of this plan she would be green with envy, but my mother is not appreciative. She sees a wheelchair as a sign of the speedy approach of Death, not as a handy way of getting out and about. And pushing the wheelchair will probably finish me off, then where shall we be?

Angela's mother across the road has a more positive attitude. She has purchased a motorised chair in which she may zip about at four miles an hour. This may sound sluggish, but it is like a rocket if you are a daughter running behind in high heels, trying to keep up over fairly rough terrain *and* keep control of the mother's dog. Ahead Angela could see the motor-chair swerving and tilting and had to stagger after it as quickly as she could to try and stop the mother tipping over into a ditch. But her mother persevered and can now play football with the dog in her garden and reach her bird-table, all in the thrilling motor-chair.

This new technology is often tricky if one is not used to it. Auntie in the North has a new adjustable armchair which she lives in. She can tip it backwards and forwards at will by pulling and pushing a knob on the arm. She is forever practising, tilting this way and that, with the armchair making whirring noises. Uncle is nearly demented by the constant noise and movement, which disturbs his peace and his telly-watching.

At least Auntie has thrown herself into a study of the new equipment, but my mother is uncooperative. This is apparently a good sign. Rosemary rushed in the other day with a newspaper article revealing that 'wilful and cantankerous' elderly persons live longer than mild and obedient ones. Our mothers are both in the first category.

And now I have ordered a stairlift for my mother against her wishes. She is in a furious bate. Deep in her heart she is convinced that the minute the stairlift is installed she will drop dead. Just her luck. Then it will have been a complete and utter waste of money.

'How much is it?' she barks crossly.

'Six hundred pounds,' I lie, halving the cost of the cheapest second-hand one.

'Bloody disgraceful,' she roars. 'You are NOT to buy one.' Were she to learn the true price she would attack the salesman or installer with her stick. I have warned them on no account to mention cost in her presence. She would rather die than pay. She even fibs to the doctor, pretending she can climb the stairs like a gazelle, but I tell on her, describing her superstitions.

'There is no connection between the installation of a stairlift and people dropping dead,' says Doctor sensibly. 'Buy the stairlift and don't use it. Unless you have to.'

This is strange logic but my mother accepts it. Perhaps it will inspire her to try out more new technology – even a wheelchair. We may yet manage our outing.

Love in the Time of Crow's-Feet

My friend Olga is at the end of a romance. It is in its death-throes. It has to be. The fellow has been leading a double life, one with Olga in town at the weekends, another with Miss X on weekdays in the country.

But it isn't only his vile duplicity that depresses her, it's her own lack of progress. Here she is, fifty-two, and still carrying on like a teenager.

'It isn't getting any better,' says Olga, drinking heavily. 'The same symptoms, the same tangled stomach, loss of weight, sobbing, waking at three a.m. with a pounding heart.' And by now she's meant to have learnt something from experience and matured.

I must say I thought her very restrained. She cried softly at dinner, was sick so politely I never even noticed and didn't even look drunk to me.

'It's just the same,' says she looking desolate, 'same blissful beginning, same hideous end.'

And same sort of chap – two-timing, mendacious, deeply in love with his work and not very generous. He doesn't seem to be doing too well for a grown-up either. He is slave to a somewhat wretched pattern – fall in love, get married, find another love, get found out, get divorced, get married again, find another, get found out. This is the fourth repeat.

'I wouldn't mind,' says Olga, 'but I've just had eight years of psychotherapy. This time I was straightforward. I asked him "would he even *countenance* two women at once?" He said no, I trusted him. I didn't keep asking. I've grown up.'

Olga had been very proud of herself. She thought this was the right person at last. But it wasn't. She had unerringly picked a stinker again.

He must have had some good points. What could they have been? Olga scrapes around and dredges up a few. 'He's a paid up member of the Labour Party,' says she wistfully, 'and Amnesty International and Greenpeace. He knows the British Museum inside out and he reads Keats like a dream.'

I'm not all that impressed by the Keats reading. I remember a chap who read Anthony Powell out loud to me in bed. My chums would have had a laugh if they could have seen it, but I simpered away and pretended I liked it. And I was quite grown up at the time.

Naturally this sort of thing is a source of amazement and consternation to friends. They listen to details of the ghastly affair, their jaws drop open, and they all cry out in unison – groups, tables, parties full of them, '*Get rid of him!* Throw him out, change the locks, we'll come round and help you. Just GET RID OF HIM.'

Olga tries ever so hard but fails repeatedly. Home she goes, full of good intentions, but a strange force drives her to the telephone. Her fingers, on automatic pilot, dart to the old familiar digits and there she is, blubbing on the phone again. Just like my seventeen-year-old daughter.

Otherwise she is tremendously mature, runs her own business, is a successful creative artist, her home is charming and tidy, her outfits tremendously stylish, her cooking is divine, her son delightful. She looks like a proper adult. It is just in this one area that she feels a failure.

And at fifty-two it's all a bit more frightening. 'Will I do it again before I die?' she wonders, looking into the cruel mirror.

'Course you will,' we all shout encouragingly, and sure enough she goes bravely off to a party and meets this fellow. They dance wildly for hours and hours and are to meet again. He seems perfectly all right to her . . .

Mother Moves In

Selling one's home at any age is fairly grim. At eighty-nine it is a nightmare. My mother is finally relinquishing her own flat in Hove, a dangerous event. The shock of it, I have heard, can knock the elderly for six. Forced to leave their homes along the A1 (blighted by the threat of a motorway), they have been dropping like flies.

Naturally my mother is in a frenzy. She cannot sleep a wink and when awake she lives and breathes Inventory. When approached by any person at any time of the day or night she will spout lists of furnishings, fittings and contents, what's to be left, what's coming here and wherever are we to put it?

'Do you want the souffle dishes?' she asks, 'I'm not leaving them.' Or the favourite armchair and sofa and candlesticks and mirror. 'And what about the white plates/plants/Magimix/carving knives?' She cannot bear to leave even the tiniest scrap of property behind.

It is a nerve-racking business. Will the buyer change her mind? She is desperately trying to beat down the price. Wait till she hears of the gargantuan charges incurred for services and repairs to the buildings. Managing Agent has obviously hired the Royal Master Craftsmen to paint the front windows.

I urge my mother not to get excited. But she is easily excited: by the dog slobbering, us leaving the lights on, the price of cheese, the relentless sound of the hoover. Meanwhile, upstairs, her teenage granddaughter is swooning with suspected glandular fever. Our home is swirling with germs and tension.

Rosemary next door comes in for a brief visit. We are all at dinner. Rosemary joins us for some apple pie and cream and high-octane Inventory. Naturally, because of the tension, we are all roaring and shouting. Rosemary stays fifteen minutes and retires shell-shocked to the safety of her own home without even finishing her pudding. She had previously thought her home rather drab and dismal, but she now sees that it is a haven of peace and culture. Its shelves of books and bits of muted but tasteful carpet and ornament makes a pleasant change from our house.

Mrs X, the buyer, rings. She has reduced her offer by several thousand. My mother is stunned. We reject Mrs X's rather saucy offer. She rings back days later with a higher one. This is playing havoc with my mother's angina. Her nerves are in shreds. She longed for a peaceful old age and is not getting one. Here is her beloved home being tossed up and down on the market like a bit of old bric-a-brac. And once it is sold she has burnt her boats. She will be stuck here forever with us.

There is nothing for it but to dress up our living room like my mother's ex-flat. Then she can pretend she's still partially there. If we can cram as much as possible into here, she will hardly realise she has moved.

Our living room is soon a replica of the Hove apartment. Not just a few items, but everything is now crammed in. We have china tea-cups and chandeliers and the gramophone throbs with rumba and paso-doble. We have the big mirror with ornate gold twirling surround, ancestral portraits and my mother's flower paintings on all walls. The ground floor is a Hove simulator.

Visitors are prone to culture shock, but my mother has

perked up tremendously. She lies on her own sofa wrapped in shawls and a rather glamorous turban, eating choc truffles, drinking pina-colada and singing, 'Ours is a nice house ours is, it's got no rats and mouses.'

This is fairly close to a compliment.

Bold Programmes

I return from my morning dog walk to find my mother glued to the television. 'They're talking about sex again,' says she, thrilled to bits. 'Yesterday it was women, today it's men. The men are better.' An Italian and an Englishman are squabbling over indigenous approaches to Love. And all this straight after breakfast.

My mother is stunned by this sudden rash of bold television programmes. Only last week we turned on the telly to watch some innocuous programme and inadvertently caught the end of another one about Men. There was a penis, growing larger by the second.

'Bloody hell,' roared my mother, shocked to the core. 'Disgusting!' She cannot get over how rude the telly has become. There was a time when one never saw anyone's bottom, male or female, back or front, upon the screen. She has had to adapt tremendously, but is learning to go with the flow.

'It's orgasms AGAIN,' she shouts this morning from her bedroom. Concern about men's health is rife and orgasms are all the rage at present and have been for some time. People are demanding them left right and centre, with sensitivity of course. No wonder men are flagging. In my mother's youth one did not talk openly about such topics.

Perhaps one should have done. It's always sensible to compare and contrast, otherwise how do you find out what you're missing? Not that I want to generalise, and millions of people probably find orgasms a walkover from the word go, but some women discover them late in life. After years of dull relationships, they find a new partner, man or woman, who rather perks things up.

This seems to happen from the late thirties onwards. 'I used to wonder what all the fuss was about,' says my friend X. For years she plodded on with this rather dreary performance with the husband, wondering what everyone else was talking about. Could it be the same activity? Then suddenly along came a new chap and the world lit up. She could scarcely move a step without an orgasm. Lucky she. Here is a pastime that can obviously improve with age.

This may in part be due to the efforts of men. They are sometimes, when older, apt to make rather more effort, if one demands it of them. My friend Fielding is forever wondering what to do for the best. People come and go with contrasting theories, rather like the Schools Inspectorate, and, unable to rely any longer on the vigour and charms of youth, he battles to keep up with them. A youth would never bother. Even if he wanted to he might not dare. This area is something of a minefield for the beginner.

Perhaps Fielding should be thrilled that he is now elderly and may, if he chooses, give up on the whole thing. No one will laugh. In later life this move is often applauded rather than sneered at. But youth has no such choice. They are under great pressure to be wild. I remember being cruelly mocked at art school in the Sixties for being rather late off the mark. There was everyone wallowing in sex and drugs, and there was I practising the piano. This was a grim time for me.

Meanwhile my mother keeps me up to date with the televised details. 'This man's twenty-three, he's never done it and he wants to wait till he's married and they're all laughing at him.' My mother laughs with them in a somewhat contemptuous and ribald way. She at least grows more and more enlightened with age.

Progress?

My friend Olivia has boldly got rid of her telly. She returned it to Radio Rentals without consulting her family, who are wandering about in a state of shock. To mollify them she has bought a dart-board. Something else for everyone to stare at, but round instead of square.

'It's heavenly without it,' says she. 'I hated it. It was ruining our lives.' She remembers her own youth as rather more uplifting. It's difficult not to hanker after things past. I deeply regret the passing of the lever pen and introduction of cartridges.

'That's a bit pretentious isn't it?' says Olivia rather harshly. It's her record-player that she misses. She spent a lot of time in her bedroom stacking her records on that little post above the deck, staring into the mirror and at the curtains. 'Curtain material tended to be narrative in those days,' says she dreamily. 'Mine had French fishermen in bellbottoms sorting little flat fish into round baskets.'

She remembers it vividly, because you had lots of time to stare at things. Or sing Bob Dylan songs in a meaningful way, unaccompanied. There wasn't much suitable for Youth on the telly, only *Peyton Place* and *Ready Steady Go*. 'And you had a ruler and logarithm books,' says Olivia wistfully.

To be rebellious she read *The Outsider* and pinned a fierce note on her door: 'The family, with its squalid secrets and hidden miseries, is the source of all our discontents.'

Her own family is now very discontented. The husband was onto Radio Rentals like a shot, reordering the telly and video for Monday. He is desperate to see *Terminator Two* again and some boxing and football. Speed and violence are a must.

I can see why Olivia is kicking up a fuss. Everything goes horribly fast nowadays, especially youth – raving, dancing, calculating, computing, microwaving, faxing, concentrating only briefly and rushing to be grown up. My daughter is forever on the go. Does she even know that her curtains are patterned? She is only motionless for long periods of time when asleep or slumped before the telly. Perhaps Olivia has deprived her family of their only frenzy-suppressant.

But progress is relentless. We are swept along with it. Rosemary next door is battling with the modern technology at her workplace. She has voice-mail. If I ring her at work I can now get her own voice telling me that she isn't there. And it's not just an answerphone. She has several deeply secret extension numbers and can *randomise* – several people at once can be told with her own voice that she isn't there. But the computer is defeating her. She has borrowed one from work to practise on in the holidays. It will not do as it is told. Rosemary is in a fury with the mouse. She wants to trample it to death. She seems unable to direct it to the correct place and press it efficiently.

'*You* come and try it,' she shouts. 'There's something wrong with it.'

There isn't. In my expert hands it works perfectly. 'Why can you do it and I can't?' Rosemary is in a dreadful temper. It soothes her to know that I too had learning difficulties with the computer. My tutor was rather harsh.

'You can't do it because you don't want to,' said he strictly, accusing me of resisting Progress. But at fifty some of us begin to question the meaning of this word. Is it leading us anywhere pleasant? Now here is Rosemary doing her best to cope with

Progress and getting nowhere. No wonder she is browned off. She's been fiddling with the computer and mouse for two days and could have written her letter fifty times over by now with a simple lever fountain pen, *and* had plenty of time to stare at the curtains.

Extravagance

Now that my mother lives on the premises she is able to observe the details of our life – a shocking thing to watch when one is eighty-nine. She is horrified by our expenditure. I have taken to lying about the cost of everything. I halve it. My mother is still outraged. There she is busy saving paper bags, Christmas cards and bits of string, then out I go and fritter money on a ready-made steamed syrup pudding.

'How much was that?' she snaps, astounded by the price. 'What did you do that for?' she roars. 'I can make one.' She stamps off to the kitchen and whips one up for tuppence.

We now buy no shop cakes or biscuits. We save egg boxes, jam jars, used stamps and old sheets. We darn clothes, reuse tea-bags and save rainwater. The house is filling with ancient scraps and rags. And we are not allowed to waste a crumb of food.

'It's from living through the war,' explains Rosemary. She has a touch of it herself, often running about the house turning the lights out after everyone.

'Blackout, blackout,' shouts her son in a mocking way. Soon my mother will be issuing ration-books to curb our somewhat profligate lifestyle. Microwave dinners, bought puddings and oven chips will be strictly limited.

My cousin in the North is under similar constraints. Her mother (my aunt) also moans on about cost. Like me, Cousin lies and halves the cost of everything. Only last week she bought Auntie some smoked salmon for a treat. Auntie commands her to shop around, but what with a full-time job and everybody's shopping to do, she hasn't the time, so as usual she halved the price.

Naturally Auntie was thrilled with the price of the salmon. She thought it such a bargain that she gave it to the cleaning lady for a present. Cousin was furious. She now has to go shopping for more salmon and tell more lies. She and I are both enmeshed in a web of deceit.

And of course I've lied like billy-o about the stairlift. It arrived today, three hours late. My other lies in bed glaring at the installers. 'I'm not a cripple,' she has shouted repeatedly. 'It's a bloody waste of money.'

I remind her that this is a recycled stairlift, second-hand, and the minute she drops dead (we have given up on euphemisms), we will sell it and get our money back. This makes her feel better. She stops snarling at the installers. For hours they fiddle about on the stairs and I must leave them there and go to work. They are under oath not to mention cost.

But I forget my keys. What luck that my mother can now answer the door. I look through the letter-box. There she is sailing downstairs on her lift. 'Ground floor, men's wear, ladies' shoes, lighting,' she calls out gaily over the grinding roar of the machinery. We are thrilled to bits, even though the lift resembles a sliding plastic lavatory and does nothing for our hallway.

My mother swans up to the lavatory on it, down again to make marmalade, up again for a rest, and down again for *Coronation Street*. She even stops mentioning The Price. Encouraged by this development, Rosemary and I take her to Marks and Spencer's for a new nightie. Every nightie is pink or cream. My mother is sickened. 'I'll look like an old woman,' she shouts. She had hoped for something more dashing – in bold colours and patterns and no teeny pink flowers.

I buy myself a brassiere and halve the price. The woman behind us in the queue hears Rosemary and me discussing my mother's attitude to spending. She joins in. Her mother will buy nothing new and lives in worn and tattered rags. 'I'll make do,' says the mother heroically. 'This will last me out.'

Obviously my mother is a spendthrift.

No Regrets

L ast week Rosemary's husband was fifty-five. He woke up looking glum and sobbed loudly over his birthday presents. Perhaps he had a delightful youth and was a handsome fellow. Apparently it is easier to grow old feeling pleasant if you have been miserable when young. Instead of missing things, you are glad to be rid of them. There is nothing like a tormented youth to make one appreciate old age.

My youth was blighted by my long nose. Fairly constant hayfever made it red and larger. Naturally I begged for some of it to be cut off, especially as girls are meant to look pretty.

'There's nothing wrong with it,' the Specialist lied through his teeth.

But now the hay-fever has gone, the nose has shrunk, and things have improved no end. I remember a ravishingly beautiful fellow student at art school who grew up to look like a potato, while a rather odd-looking chum of mine now looks strikingly attractive. So for those who look rather odd when young, and had a plain or rather grim physiognomy, age makes little difference. Things can only improve. People who in their youth were stunningly attractive perhaps ought to be thrilled that they ever had it at all. They have only lost what the great number of the human race never have possessed, said Dr Johnson rather strictly, and he ought to know.

The ageing process has rather depressed my mother. Both she and my father were strikingly glamorous in their youth. For some years now she has not been keen on looking in the mirror. 'Ugh,' she moans, 'I look shocking.'

'She thinks she's Jane Fonda,' my father used to mumble in a mocking way, and then he covered the walls of the lavatory with pictures of Princess Diana. In his old age he spent quite a lot of time in the lavatory. My mother retaliated with pictures of Kilroy.

They seem to have forgotten the horrors of adolescence: spots, school, exams, being embarrassed at parties, battling with parents and dealing with boyfriends. I remember one particularly bleak vignette from my youth – a New Year's party at a squat in Tooting with purple walls, red light bulbs and someone being sick out of the upstairs window. This was a low point, but all in all the Sixties was not a period which I am desperate to relive. Nowadays I am far more selective about outings.

Rosemary and I and Olga are looking forwards rather than backwards and planning for old age constructively, so that we don't end up moping around looking in mirrors noticing turkey necks and senile warts. We and a few other chums will leave or sell all our homes, purchase a large rambling property, divide it up into flatlets, and have a shared staff: nurse, cook, driver, gardener, and manage that way. It will be much cheaper than having one each. And anyway we shall have no choice. National Health and Community Care will have gone zooming down the drain, and if we have to spend all our savings and pensions caring for ourselves then we might as well club together and choose somewhere pleasant.

It won't quite be a commune, just a shared garden and shared dining room optional, but with separate quarters. My dog will not be allowed in Rosemary's bit. Then we can all be driven in the communal minibus to the cinema and file out with our Zimmer frames to see something classy at the Renoir, trying to keep the minds stimulated, or something at the Odeon to keep us awake.

On birthdays one will be surrounded by chums, and not have to do any cooking or washing up. Bliss. Hopefully nobody will be crying over their presents.

Parking Mad

Transport for the elderly can be rather problematic. It is not easy getting my mother to the bank. Most banks are on High Streets, protected from the immobile customer by double yellow lines and armies of traffic wardens. So for weeks I have postponed this outing, but my mother is dead keen to go.

At last we find ourselves on the High Street outside the chocolate shop. My mother is desperate for chocolate gingers. I am to dash in and buy them while she waits in the car. We are in a parking bay on a red route, but is it safe? On which side of the road may we park today and for how long?

'It's all right anywhere,' roars my mother with confidence. 'I've got my yellow badge.' She has forgotten that this is not Hove, but London, where life is brutal and harsh, criminals abound and law enforcement agencies are ruthless and sometimes even privatised. They know that my mother may be a vandal in disguise.

I rush to buy the chocs and return to find my mother chatting to a lady traffic warden in a friendly way about our Bank Problem. The warden assures her that we may park outside the bank freely with our disabled badge.

My mother is thrilled and now cannot be stopped. She must go the bank. 'We can park there at any time,' says she defiantly. 'That nice lady warden said so.'

We go the very next day. Imagine our surprise as we stagger from the bank, to see a warden writing out a ticket. But this one isn't a charming lady. It is a white, pinched-face youth determined to book us. Blindly following the Nice Lady's instructions, we had failed to notice that one may not park here after four o'clock. It is now quarter past. Forty pounds fine.

My mother pleads and begs Pinchface to stop but he couldn't care less. Were she to have a heart attack on the spot he would still issue his ticket, but my mother will try.

'Give up,' I yell coarsely from the car. 'You won't get anywhere. He couldn't give a *!*!*.' I am right, but it takes my mother some time to realise this. She repeats the instructions of the charming lady warden, she describes her infirmities, but to no avail, and our day is ruined.

Luckily we do not often need to visit High Streets. My mother's lunch club is out of town and one can park in a carefree way. Bliss. Only this week I cannot take her. My car is in the garage. Never mind, we'll book a taxi. My mother has a Taxi Card. We book it for 9.15 a.m.

Foolish innocents. The taxi fails to arrive. There is my mother, woken at dawn, struggling for two hours to get ready, waiting in her best clothes for her favourite weekly outing, and no taxi. I ring the taxi firm with these heart-rending details. They are unmoved.

'We haven't got one yet,' says the lady in charge, probably accustomed to moaning pensioners. 'We don't know when we'll have one. It does say on your card that this is not a guaranteed service.'

Transport facilities are obviously something of a lottery for the elderly. Rosemary's eighty-four-year-old mother is taken to and from her day centre by coach. The coach collects people alphabetically, which means driving all over London in large zig-zags, frequently passing within a whisker of Rosemary's mother's street. She begs the driver to drop her there, but he won't. She must zig-zag London for hours because her name begins with W.

Today I leave my mother waiting, chicly dressed, for her taxi, and stamp off for a dog walk. She is still there when I come back, resigned to her fate. I am in a foaming temper, but my mother is calm. She has become accustomed to transport cock-ups and waiting about like a bit of lost baggage. It is a part of growing old.

Legs

Sightseeing can be rather gruelling when one is over fifty, standing about staring at things, so when Rosemary invited me on a tour of the Houses of Parliament last week, I declined to go, much as I long to see our leaders in action. Rosemary went with her mother, family and chums and came back exhausted. What luck that I stayed at home.

Her tour guide in the House of Lords had been extremely bossy and would allow no one to sit down unless a Peer of the Realm or eldest son of a Peer of the Realm. An elderly lady with angina had the audacity to sit and was sharply reprimanded.

'Madam,' said the Guide fiercely, 'I shall have to ask you to vacate the Chamber.'

It is a long tour and once on it there seemed to be no escape. 'Our varicose veins were beginning to stand out like mad,' moaned Rosemary, but the Guide had no mercy, and as they trudged wearily round, he fired questions at them.

'Now,' he snapped, 'is the Guinea still legal tender? Why didn't the Navy have to swear allegiance to the Queen?'

Rosemary has never been keen on Trivial Pursuit. She longed to join another tour group. If she listened carefully she could hear the guides from the other six groups, which she much preferred. One explained why one toe of Winston Churchill's statue is shiny and the other dull. Rosemary was riveted. Rebelliously she tried to join this group, but the Guide spotted her at once.

'Will you please rejoin your own group, Madam,' he barked strictly, and Rosemary crept back to the questioning and standing.

The only person who had a really pleasant and comfortable time was Rosemary's mother, who was luckily issued with a wheelchair, forever being trundled off to exciting alternative exits, entrances and lifts and able to sit down throughout. This tour was a joy to her. There are obvious benefits to being very old rather than just a bit old like Rosemary and her chums, who staggered round with their veins throbbing for hours.

There is nothing worse, when one's legs are beginning to weaken, than to have to dawdle about looking at things. It gives me a fearful ache up the legs and round the waist. Sometimes I have been forced to sit on the ground in a public place, embarrassing and enraging my daughter.

Striding along briskly is all right, but not shuffling and standing. I can no longer stand chatting at parties. I must sit down and be isolated. And perhaps this is why shopping has rather lost its charm for me. I cannot bear the hovering, wandering and choosing, especially of clothes. Consequently I dress mainly in rags or by mail order. The result has been rather dull. Luckily I have just found a charming second-hand clothes shop where one can sit down, chat, and have a coffee or even a gin and tonic while choosing garments. To my mind, this is the way to shop.

At least Rosemary saw one strikingly impressive person on her outing – Betty Boothroyd. 'She looked very dashing,' said Rosemary, 'and slimmer than I expected.' As B. Boothroyd swept by in the Speaker's Procession, gentlemen removed their hats and her train was held up elegantly by a fellow in gaiters. For a few heavenly moments while admiring this performance, Rosemary completely forgot about her legs.

Presumably Betty Boothroyd does this frequently, a brisk processional stride, then a long sit-down, enhanced in this case by being able to call large numbers of unruly men to order.

Rosemary and I feel that this is what older women want, just in case anyone wants to know.

Problem Age

The elderly are now considered to be something of a nuisance. We have a glut of them. A glut of anything can be a problem – butter, babies, rabbits, grey squirrels – and so are the elderly. They need new teeth, new glasses, new hips, extra heating, extra nursing, extra medicine, fewer stairs, mobility and attendance allowances and pensions. This is a problem age.

There are other problem ages: infancy, childhood, adolescence, adulthood, mid-life crisis, menopause – but as the elderly (fifty-plus) now form the bulk of the population, they are the biggest problem – a huge parasite or drone group burdening the young.

Naturally we do not subscribe to this view in our house, but it is a fairly common view of the elderly. It has been for some time. I spotted something similar in Nascher's *Geriatrics* (1914). 'Their appearance is generally unaesthetic, their actions objectionable, their very existence often an incubus on those who in a spirit of humanity take upon themselves the care of the aged.'

This makes the future seem rather drear. No one is keen to become an incubus, sucking the life and money out of younger beings. And this general view has filtered through to my mother. She expresses it in her glummer moments, when *Coronation Street* and bridge games are days away and her arthritis is flourishing. 'I'm a nuisance wherever I go,' says she, dragging herself back to bed in despair. 'I'm no use to anyone.'

But she doesn't have to be. We are forever telling her. Rules differ according to location. In India the elderly feel that they have a right to be looked after by their own children. It is just repayment for the effort spent in their own youth on producing and bringing up these creatures. Old age is their turn to sit about doing nothing and being pandered to and cared for. Ideally. They are to live with their children and be looked after in a pleasant way. They do not expect to be answered back, but deferred to and respected.

As a reciprocal courtesy, the older relatives, although resident in the younger family's home, mind their own business and do not interfere or complain about the cooking. Spiritually they are to be off, especially the men, towards the next life, detached from mundane domestic worries and so able to contemplate God. They are not expected to live alone. Independence is not particularly admired, as in parts of the Western world.

Unfortunately not everyone comes up to scratch in these roles, even in India. The children may be selfish and lazy, desire for money may poison things, the elderly may not mind their own business or be very ill for a very long time, and nastiness may reign, just as it often does in the West.

I must admit that we fail in a number of areas. Household standards are somewhat slapdash, manners sometimes poor, and try as she might, my mother cannot refrain from criticism. But we are all improving.

Some people always knew that old age is an achievement. Wilfred Pickles and his wife Mable used to on their radio show. 'How old are you Mr/Mrs X?' Wilfred would ask.

'Seventy-nine,' said Mr or Mrs X proudly.

'Seventy-nine? Isn't that wunderful? Give him/her a big hand everybody.' Loud applause from the studio audience. Just for being seventy-nine.

Pity no one has come along to replace Wilfred.

Street Foolish

I am driving along in the car with my daughter when I spot a very oddly dressed girl. Is it a girl? I can hardly make her out. She is swamped in huge clothes – a giant-size sheepskin jacket, a flying hat with mammoth ear-flaps, huge boots and massive trousers. She looks furious.

'Look at that girl,' I instruct my daughter while we sit at the traffic-lights. 'Look at that hat.' I point one finger discreetly while holding the wheel.

'Don't point,' commands my daughter with her mouth shut, pretending not to look or speak. 'Are you mad? That's a Ragga Girl. Do *not* stare at her.'

Perhaps the ragga girl has a machine-gun hidden in her coat. 'Why not?' I nag on relentlessly. 'Why dress like that if she doesn't want to be stared at?'

'You are so stupid,' hisses my daughter, pale with fright. 'Will you just shut up.' She stares straight ahead and speaks with her mouth closed. That way the girl will never guess we are related.

Luckily the lights change and we whiz off, but I obviously know little of street life. There I sit at home, night after night while the daughter is out, worrying and imagining all the terrible things that might happen to her, when really it is me who is more at risk. She knows how to avoid provoking the more sensitive thugs when out and about, but I don't know who to look at and who not to look at, who to speak to and how, and when to mind my own business. I am street foolish.

Only the other day I reprimanded some children in a small local park for wrenching the trees to bits and splodging obscene graffiti all over the benches, but their mothers rose up to defend them and I narrowly escaped a punch on the nose.

Perhaps it is wise for me to avoid small parks. I am forever coming across vandals and telling them off. It does no good at all. They become ruder and vandalise with renewed vigour. But if left alone they would continue vandalising anyway. I cannot win, especially with the mothers supporting the vandals.

'Silly cow,' shouted the mothers cheerily as I disappeared in a bate. 'Go on,' they called encouragingly to their children, 'go and break some more trees.'

This was a depressing incident. Living in town can be a thrill a minute, but at times like this it tends to cast me into a glump. Vandals, beggars and the homeless and rootless are on the increase. I seem able to do nothing about the vandals. I can, however, distribute money to people sitting about the streets asking for it. This makes an outing, even to the shops, rather expensive.

My father was always rather critical of such donations. He suspected all beggars of having holiday homes in Spain, or private suites at the Curzon Hotel. What's more, they were collected from their begging pitch at the end of the day by a chauffeur-driven Daimler and taken to a secret luxury address, where they counted up the immense takings collected from mugs like me. This was my father's firm belief, but I do not go along with it.

Neither did Rosemary, until this week. Being a social work lecturer, she tends to be liberal rather than cynical, but yesterday she came home from Sainsbury's in a roaring temper. There she was, standing in a queue behind this young, poor-looking girl with a baby. All the girl had in her basket was a huge sack of potatoes and two packets of beans, and she couldn't even afford to pay for that. She needed another 8 pence.

Michele Hanson

Rosemary gave it to her. Other ladies in the queue and the girl's friend tutted and clucked with disapproval. In fact it wasn't 8 pence. Rosemary had misheard. It was 18 pence. Rosemary handed over a 20-pence piece. More clucking. Then the girl paid, pocketed Rosemary's 2 pence change and made off cheerily without saying thank-you.

'What about my 2 pence?' Rosemary roared after her, rather unnerved by the tutting and clucking and lack of gratitude. Even a liberal likes a bit of gratitude.

'She always gets away with it,' said the girl's friend, laughing at Rosemary as they buzzed off.

Naturally Rosemary went home in a bate. On her way she passed a *Big Issue* vendor and refused to buy a copy. 'They're all the same,' she thought, soured by her experience and feeling foolish. She needs a few car rides with my daughter.

Bad Temper

I seem to be growing increasingly bad-tempered with age, especially about the house. It is choc-full of things that annoy: the washing-up, clothing, food, hoover and all the other machinery and household equipment.

Luckily I am not alone. My friend Sylvia, a little older than myself, became so infuriated with a milk carton that refused to open that she hurled it into the sink. Naturally it burst, spurting milk everywhere. Sylvia then had to clean the whole sink area, which drove her almost to the verge of madness. All she had wanted was a plain cup of tea.

It is these deceptively simple tasks that do it. Only yesterday I tried to water the front garden by pulling the hose through via a back window. I went outside, pushed it through the window, ran round to the front, pulled it to the garden, ran to the back, turned on the water, ran to the front, watered, ran back, turned it off. But meanwhile, a fierce gale blowing through from the back had blown down my mother's dried flower arrangement and the living room floor was showered with bits of petal and stalk. This meant a giant hoovering task for me, and the hoover was two floors up.

I have heard that other people mellow out with age, but Sylvia and I are not doing this. These fiddling things about the home are not what we want to be doing at our age. They take the rest of your life away, and all the while the washing-up piles up mouldering in the sink, breakfast, lunch, tea and dinner come round again and again, and the bit at the back of the fridge keeps filling with water and flooding and I have nothing to poke it with. Meanwhile another day has zinged by, another step closer to the grave, involving nothing pleasant.

Rosemary and my mother find cooking tremendously relaxing, but I am sick of it after all these years – the peeling, chopping, washing, shopping, selecting and planning. I shout loudly at the potato-peeler, which keeps twizzling round the wrong way.

Only one thing stops me bellowing – the dog. It is fearfully upset by my temper. It hides away in corners and cringes. It has digestive problems and the tension is probably playing havoc with its bowels. It paws the air in a desperate way and I am shamed into silence.

Of course my shouting and stamping about is generally frowned upon. Only when one is much older is this sort of behaviour acceptable. If I do it people mumble 'menopause' and look away, but if my mother does it, they gaze at her fondly. At ninety one may apparently display the vilest of tempers and no one minds. I am rather envious.

I was buying some delightful T-shirts last week from the favourite second-hand shop which serves gin and tonic, and ran out to the car to show my mother the colour selection. Rather foolishly I disclosed the price. My mother could no longer remain passively in the car. She burst into the shop in my wake and fiercely reprimanded the shop-owner.

'They're only five pounds in Marks and Spencer's,' my mother shouted. 'Bloody disgusting waste of money.'

Naturally I apologised to the saleslady, whose T-shirts were French and rather classy. 'She's ninety in a few weeks,' said I, cringing.

'Oh, that's all right then,' said the saleslady, laughing in a relaxed way.

Here is something else to look forward to. Only another thirty-seven years and I can be as rude and grumpy as I like.

A Horse, A Horse

My friend Olivia tells me that her sister, aged forty-four, has recently accepted redundancy rather eagerly, and thrown herself into horse-riding and millinery with great intensity. The sister is on the verge of a new life.

Obviously, a large redundancy payment is something of a plus when starting a new life, but new starts seem to be rather popular for people of our age, redundancy payment or not. The financial adviser wants to be a gardener, the gardener up the road wants to be a singer, my barrister friend is learning to be a psychoanalyst, and Olga, browned off with pottery, has started to paint her interior walls in such a stunning fashion that her whole home is now one giant art work.

'Call in the Designers' Guild,' we all shout. Olga has obviously discovered a new talent. At fifty-one she has burst out into a new field of creativity. The world of interior design is her oyster.

I notice that several famous models have turned to animal welfare in later life and I am now oddly devoted to my dog. What I would really like to do is to rescue orang-utans from captivity and return them to the wild, but would I be able to cope with life in the jungle – the insects, the absence of lovely clean indoor lavatories? So for now I have taken up the cello. People often do in later life, says my teacher (who wants to give up teaching and open a cake shop in the North). She has an even older student than me. Our sight may be failing, our brains crystallised and sinews fairly rigid, but we are still progressing.

And teachers often welcome mature students. They are more dedicated. I was a mature student at thirty-three. Having been rebellious in my youth and stamped off to art school at sixteen, I tried university in later life.

There were three other women of my age in class and we all sat in the front row, listening attentively, writing reams of notes, being polite and eagerly answering questions. Meanwhile all the normal students, eighteen-plus, crawled into lectures, lounged about at the back of class smoking and participated minimally. They perhaps thought us grown-ups in swots' row quite sickening. There we were with our hands shooting up, thrilled to bits by Chaucer and his contemporaries.

The barrister friend learning to be a psychoanalyst is not such a popular pupil. She tends to challenge the rules of her institution rather boldly. This gets right up her tutor's nose. Perhaps he should give up and turn to gardening. It seems to be an absolute favourite. Now that Rosemary's children have grown up and more or less left home, she is nurturing her garden like mad.

And this year I attended the Chelsea Flower Show for the first time. It was thronged with women of my age and older. They were tremendously sprightly. I found shuffling around in a crowd of thousands rather exhausting and soon had to lie down on a lawn for fish and chips and a rest, so perhaps gardening is not for me. But I do have one major ambition left – to have a horse. I had begun to despair about this one, but I hear that a very old chum of mine, now fifty-two, has recently bought one, *and* she has five dogs and two goats. Naturally people begged her not to do it at her age, but she went ahead and is now a happy woman, galloping over hills and along beaches up in the North. There is still life after fifty years in London.

Women Behaving Badly

I notice that most of the people in my road have grown-up homes. Rosemary and I feel that we haven't. It is a pretty poor show to be fifty-three and still not have a tidy adult home. My mother is fearfully embarrassed. She will not invite friends to tea. She feels that she is inviting them to student lodgings.

Together Rosemary and I stare glumly out of our first-floor bedroom windows at the houses on the other side of the road, where people have lovely tidy living rooms and kitchen extensions, indicating a sophisticated visual sense. Our homes are not like this.

It is too late now to try and emulate the neighbours. We are too set in our ways. We must stick with the eccentric look and just exaggerate what we have already. Then people will think it deliberate, rather than unavoidable weakness. So Rosemary's home is to have an intellectual air, walled with books, and mine will be crammed with more and more succulents, like a charmingly orchestrated jungle instead of an ordinary mess.

Anyway, a smart home is not always all it's cracked up to be. It brings its own problems. My friend Olivia inherited a very fine family house in west London when she married – her husband's home. There it was, beautifully decorated and furnished in an adult way, ready for her to move in. Then one evening she was sitting in it with her husband and new baby watching the telly. The baby fell asleep and they went on watching the telly, on and on, watching and watching.

Suddenly a terrible realisation swept over Olivia. There was no one to tell them to stop watching and go to bed. No Mummy to come in and shout, 'turn it off.' They could go on and on watching all night. Olivia was now the grown-up in charge. This was not a pleasant feeling.

There are those who long to grow up and take charge, but Olivia and I find it rather a struggle. It is even difficult for me to keep my voice down to a mature-sounding level. If I don't keep a sharp check on it, it leaps up an octave, sounding rather like a ten-year-old with adenoid problems. This is a tremendous disadvantage in the world of work. It often happens in the presence of my mother. Heaven knows what that means. Up goes the voice and my mother assumes her role of grown-up in command.

'Have you put a scarf on?' she bellows as I leave the house with a chum. 'It's bloody freezing, you'll both catch cold. And lock the car doors from the inside.'

I am still her baby, but I am my daughter's mother, two difficult roles to combine. No wonder I have a squeaky voice and collect tadpoles.

There are ways and ways of looking at childish behaviour in adults. Some people find it refreshing, others find it sickening. Not that I want to sound strident or bitter, but it is often more acceptable in men. A woman who cracks jokes, pulls faces and plays with toy trains and boats is not highly thought of. I have received a certain amount of criticism for playing wildly on the floor with my dog and its squeaking hedgehog.

A certain degree of serenity is obviously called for if one is to pass as a proper adult, but this morning Rosemary and I squabbled over some chocolates. I took her favourite. We will never make the grade. Fortunately I still have my Mummy here telling me to turn the lights off.

Trail of Hatred

My friend Olga was terribly upset last week. She suddenly discovered that someone she had always thought reasonably pleasant actually hated her like poison. What could she have done to merit such loathing? We couldn't work it out. Probably some ancient and complex jealousy had got the woman seething.

Luckily I was able to reassure Olga that one surprise enemy was a very low score. I have notched up at least five. Perhaps there are more that I don't know about, but at least five persons that I have known think me unspeakably vile. I'm not always quite sure why. I hear that in one household, my name may not be mentioned, even sixteen years after The Row. My score did get up to seven, but I managed to chum up with a couple of them again, which brings my score down to five.

This seems to be fairly average. My friend Andrea, while studying psychoanalysis, has managed to infuriate her analyst and her tutor, who surely ought to know better. Analyst shakes with rage and Tutor groans and averts his head as she enters the room, which brings Andrea's score up to five.

So if Olga has got through fifty-one years of life with only one enemy, she is doing awfully well. Compared to her I have left a giant trail of hatred behind me.

Perhaps it runs in the family. These sulks go on and on, gathering strength with time. My Auntie and Uncle never spoke to each other for twenty years while living in the same house, so my father never again spoke to Uncle, his brother-in-law, or his niece, or my other auntie, who was unkind to the first auntie, despite her suffering. And the first auntie wouldn't ever speak to two of her sisters, or to her grandchildren, although they came knocking at her door begging to be friends. Compared to Auntie, Olga deserves a place in heaven.

In a family like ours it's difficult to keep track of whom one is and isn't allowed to speak to. I recently chummed up with one of my banned cousins at a funeral. My mother was sickened by my duplicity. And there are some people who cannot be mentioned without my mother affecting nausea.

This is no way to carry on. I am aiming to get my score down to three before I die. I would like to make it nought, but I think those three are fairly determined. Meanwhile, on the plus side, I do have other chums that I have known for decades and we still like each other. Only the other day a friend came round whom I have known since I was eight.

In those days we had very few rows, but lots of thrilling moneymaking schemes: the ginger beer factory in her dad's garage, the mouse-breeding area in our shed, the perfume from rose petals and the duck egg sales. Sadly, the ginger beer exploded, the mouse-breeding got rather out of hand, the rose petals rotted and my mother cruelly ate my ducks while I went on a brief holiday. But despite all this stress, we never fell out.

Little did we know that all around us the grown-ups were sulking, behaving badly and leading tortured lives. Mrs X down the road stalked my father, Mr Y had an affair, Auntie fiddled Grandma's will and enraged my mother. The grown-up world was choc-a-bloc with loathing. It obviously still is.

The Wedding

I am to go to my friend's daughter's wedding in Cornwall. I don't really want to go. I feel something of a social outcast at weddings, having never had one myself. This has been a great disappointment to my mother and also something of a disappointment to my daughter, who has always longed to be a bridesmaid. This would have meant a dazzling new dress for her. I have ruined their dreams.

Should I ever marry, I fancy *The Arrival of the Queen of Sheba* for my entrance music. Meanwhile I shall stand sadly in the church, a fallen woman and infidel, dreaming a hopeless dream and trying not to cry.

No wonder I am not keen to go. *And* I will be leaving my mother, my daughter and the dog behind. Will they behave properly and look after one another? Naturally I set off in a glum and apprehensive mood with my escort and eat a rather large and comforting picnic on the train. I arrive in Cornwall and eat a large and comforting crab salad in the pub. Then off to the dread church.

Here are people I haven't seen for fifteen years with their grown-up children whom I can hardly recognise. Who is the elegant young woman looking vaguely familiar with her baby and her sister? Here and there are separated parents with new partners and new children, half-brothers and sisters, step-fathers and stepmothers. And here comes the bride, a vision of loveliness in cream lace and satin with pink roses in her golden hair, looking radiant.

What a relief that I don't like the hymns, babies are squawking fairly continuously throughout the service so I can hardly hear the words, and they are modern anyway. All of which stops me crying. Apparently Jesus visited this church personally. Whatever was he doing in southern Cornwall?

Then on to the reception, in a white marquee next to a castle on a low cliff overlooking a bay. The sun shines, a seal comes swimming along, it is fairyland. Then the champagne, a huge dinner, more crab, speeches, fireworks, pudding with chocolate sauce and clotted cream, more pudding. For some reason I eat continuously. This wedding is heavenly. I even have a wild dance, which is soon curtailed by asthma. I can now only dance in short bursts – a dance, a sit-down, a wheeze, another dance.

Then up in the morning for full English breakfast and back on the train, to our house for lamb stew prepared by my mother, a tempestuous row between my mother and my daughter, then up at three o'clock in the morning to be violently sick.

There is obviously only so much I can eat and do at my age without fairly horrible repercussions. And as I lie recovering from my weekend of excess I remember who the girl with the baby was – a pupil in the third year of a comprehensive in which I taught in my twenties. She and her twin sister were two of the school horrors, in a class of thirteen-year-old teacher-demolishers. To enter the 3C classroom was to enter purgatory. What luck that I am no longer a tormented student music-teacher. Even with the asthma, violent sickness and wedding phobia, there are enormous benefits to being fifty-three.

Plague Week

This has been plague week in our house. I have been sick, my daughter has been sick, the chap I went to the wedding with has been sick and the dog has been sick. This was a nightmare for my mother, with her bedroom right next to the bathroom. She was wakened at three a.m. by vile roaring noises and pitiful moans, which went on until lunch-time.

It is worrying when your primary carer is flat-out on the bathroom floor or in bed semi-conscious. And our helpful neighbour Rosemary was away on holiday *and* it was bank holiday.

Then my mother was struck down. Her right eye began to hurt like billy-o and went blind. 'Get her to the eye hospital at once,' said the doctor over the phone, 'if you want to save the sight in that eye.' Luckily Olga was able to whiz my mother to hospital in her car.

But what if the eye could not be repaired? What if the other eye packed up as well? What would my mother do, unable to read, watch telly or look at the flowers? These were my horrid thoughts as I lay weakly in bed. I imagined my mother groping her way round the house, tripping over the dog and other piles of mess. I would be forever tidying and my mother would have to learn to love Radio 4 and live without watching *Coronation Street*.

Luckily none of this happened. Olga and she were back in a trice with eye-drops, but imagine the flap in our house. My mother wished to contact Social Services at once. This had set her panicking about the future. What if I am ill again? She needs an assistant to call on when I malfunction.

I ring Social Services again. They heard of us months ago when we were all healthy and have already allocated us some-one. She will ring tomorrow. She phones while I am out walking the dog for ten minutes. How did my mother not hear? She was clutching the new cordless phone, bought for just such emergencies. I ring back but Social Worker is now away for a few days.

My mother is ninety next week. Will she live to meet the social worker? I hear from Rosemary, who is a member of this profession, that people have been known to die waiting. Their file has been labelled 'dormant' or 'inactive', and left resting while other more critical clients are being dealt with. Sometimes the 'dormant' person fades away unnoticed.

But I am being unjust after a difficult week. The population is getting bigger, madder and sicker and Social Services are overworked and desperate, yet despite all this they have flooded round to our house and fixed lavatory seats, wall rails, Meals on Wheels and Mobile Library. And within days someone else appears to assess my mother's needs, which have increased.

I can tell her what they are, easy: a new, immaculately tidy ground-floor apartment with bidet, relays of polite and high quality bridge players, a handsome, rich and charming husband for me, and most of all, a new body for herself. Meanwhile, we may have a Personal Care Assistant twice a week.

I hear there's a bit of a waiting list.

Arrival of the Wheels

I pick my mother up from her day centre on a sunny afternoon. She is cheesed off. The fish at lunch was smelly, a loud, rude and bossy man ruined her bridge game, she is hot and worn out and cannot wait to get home and lie down in a slump.

But I have a surprise for her – I have hired a wheelchair. I feel that a ride through the scented azaleas of Kenwood would perk her up no end. I point to the wheelchair folded up in the back of the car.

'Surprise!' I trill, but my mother only groans. To her the wheelchair is the end of the road.

'I'm not a bloody cripple,' she roars. Even after one year in North London, she has learnt nothing of PC. But I am ruthless. We will go on just a tiny walk through a shady and perfumed grove while the dog has its afternoon outing.

We try the wheelchair. Even my mother is vaguely excited. We trundle down a drive, soothed by a light breeze and shaded by various greens, then reach the rhododendrons and azaleas. The heavenly colours and divine scent cure my mother's dumps. It is difficult to feel crabby in this delightful venue, and in her seventy years in London, my mother has never seen it. She is entranced. We have tea and scones admiring the view of rolling lawns and glittering lakes.

Only one thing mars our outing. It is hell pushing my mother up slopes. There is rather a steep one back up to the car park. There I am, sweating, red in the face, my hair stuck to my head

71

and getting nowhere. And just as my mother is about to get out and walk, a very handsome man stops to help us. My mother is thrilled. Not only have we reached the car park, but we may also have met a Prince Charming for me. It is her desperate wish that I should meet such a person before she dies. Then she may hand over responsibility and relax at last.

Encouraged by this thrilling walk, Rosemary and I decide to push my mother round a small nearby park the next day. Easier said than done. There are scarcely any ramps on the pavements. If there's one on one side of the road, then there isn't a matching one opposite. How are we to cross roads? How is anyone in a wheelchair to get anywhere?

And then there are holes, ledges, dips, rubbish bags, builders' equipment and barriers. One outing with a wheelchair and we are turned into militants. No wonder the disabled are carrying on. I am in a raging temper after one brief walkie.

Undeterred, Rosemary and I take my mother on a giant tour of the Heath for her ninetieth birthday surprise. Between the two of us we can manage it, up and down the hills, rattling over the stony paths. It is heavenly adventure, except that the chair is uncomfortable, my mother's hip hurts, and Rosemary and I are completely knackered by home time.

We now both need a wheelchair.

Cleaning Lady

For months my mother has been nagging for a cleaning lady. She cannot physically do the cleaning herself, my cleaning is sub-standard, and my mother, feeling that she lives in a mire of filth, is sinking into gloom. She likes a gleaming tidy home, kept in order by a cleaning lady, who preferably works like a demon and never takes tea-breaks. She is a ruthless employer.

Naturally I am not keen to have a cleaning lady. I feel that I shall be committing an innocent person to hours of labour in a slave galley with my mother as harsh overseer, just because of my own sluttishness and inadequacies. Furthermore, slave wages will be paid as my mother is not au fait with the idea of a minimum wage and doesn't give a fig for socialist values or the new wave of middle-class guilt.

But she is determined. If I won't get a cleaning lady, then she will. As I push her along in the dread wheelchair she calls out loudly to all the local shopkeepers, 'DO YOU KNOW A CLEANING LADY?' She describes her misfortune at having to live in a slum and begs movingly for help.

Now at last she has got lucky. The greengrocer knows one. Kathy. In fact she has just passed by. She is at this very moment in the next-door launderette. He rushes off to find her. Imagine the excitement. My mother is thrilled to bits. Her life in the rubbish tip is almost over. Her saviour is only seconds away.

Soon Kathy appears. A brief interview is conducted on the pavement. She will come to look at our house later this evening. But will she want to work there? Should I quickly whirl round cleaning, polishing and tidying things up? Will she enter, shout 'Aaargh,' and run away, rejecting my home as a workplace and leaving my mother in Hades?

Were my mother not present I would tend to go for casual timekeeping, long tea-breaks and chats about personal lives. I have had a cleaning lady in the past, but her private life was so gripping, mine such a mess and she and I in such a state that the tea-breaks rather dominated things. Her husband was a batterer, her daughter captured by Yardies, and she in need of secret lifts to meet her lover, who would wait a few streets away. Then I had my relationship with a mendacious two-timing fellow to drone on about. Every week we had another thrilling instalment. We had scarcely a moment left for work.

My mother would never have allowed things to slide like that. She carries out inspections and issues strict instructions without the weeniest twinge of guilt. She was born to rule.

What luck that Kathy and my mother fall for each other at first sight. My mother arises from her gloom-induced lethargy. They whiz about chatting, tidying and having the odd rapid slurp of tea on the wing. Meanwhile I can sit in my room undisturbed, drowning in mess, racking the empty brain or fiddling away with another useless bit of prose. We are happy at last. More or less.

Baby Dog

My dog has a chest infection. Although it is nearly nine and weighs four and a half stone I call it my Baby Dog and coddle it while it is poorly. Many friends and neighbours are absolutely sickened by this. They have no idea that I am planning to buy another dog, or even two, when this one has passed away.

I shan't tell anyone. They are bound to say 'Don't do it,' but it is only now, in late middle age, that one realises how perfect a dog can be. Perhaps by this time we have a more accurate picture of the world and its disappointments.

Looking back over the broken marriages, shattered relationships, dull partners, difficult children, periods of desolation and gruelling careers or lack of them, one can see the merits of sticking to dogs and cats. It is a viable option. The young may sneer, but from where they are, the future is full of possibilities – romance, sex, thrills, adventure, freedom, children and happy families. They would never imagine that a dog might be a sensible choice, and a brave one.

My friend Sylvia bought a Boxer puppy when she was seventy-one. Of course everyone moaned on at her about it – she was mad to do it at her age/what if she was ill?/died?/could no longer walk?/wanted to go on holiday? But she cleverly ignored them and bought one – a wild, galloping Boxer, and together we stagger around the Heath with our dogs, keeping fit.

My friend Jim, however, has unwisely refused to buy another dog following the death of old Bessie. He no longer has cause to walk anywhere and his stomach is growing larger by the day. Try as he might, he cannot reduce its size. His asthma is worse and a nebuliser looms in the corner of his living room. If only he had a large dog again, he too would be striding about daily, breathing deeply and looking trim, as we do.

He has no excuse. A man is less subject to mockery than a woman. One man and his dog is generally seen as an attractive and almost romantic unit. A woman with a dog is not. In view of this, my friend in the North is a brave woman. She has even more pets that I first thought: four dogs, two goats, six cats, one cockatiel and a horse, and talks of rides and legovers in a rather robust way. What's more, her mare is now having a baby. A large and dashing young stallion broke into her field and this is the result.

'I'm to become a mummy in six weeks,' says she, terrified. Studying her wrinkles last night in the magnifying mirror, she noticed a frill of new grey hairs round her temple. No wonder. She is reading about 'signs to look for up to the birth of the new child', and plans to camp out in the field at nights with thermos and sandwiches playing midwife.

This makes me into a raging moderate. Perhaps my friend is dealing with the 'empty nest' syndrome. When one lives in a rather dramatic household as we do, an empty nest can seem a delightful prospect, even more so with an extra dog or baby horse in it.

Funeral Plans

My mother is planning her funeral. She wants it all nicely organised in advance so that I won't be flapping around screaming and crying and not knowing what to do when the time comes. She is to be cremated, but where and by whom? Here or in Hove? Then where shall I scatter the ashes?

I *do* have it organised, but she is still anxious. This week she is ninety and time's winged chariot is roaring up the garden path. 'This is my last birthday,' she cries in a voice of doom. 'I won't be here next year.'

'You've been saying that for years Grandma,' says my daughter airily. Perhaps half a dozen birthdays and Christmases have been Last Ones. There have been last Springs, last Summers and last lots of sticky buds. Now here we are at the ninetieth of everything.

People stare admiringly at my mother. 'She's ninety,' I say.

'Never./Would you believe it?/I hope I look like that at her age.'

My mother isn't so thrilled. This is the time of life when the body really starts playing up. It's not just a few wrinkles, warts and saggy bits, but the insides falling apart – the bowels, bones, heart, lungs, and the trowelful of pills to keep everything going.

All her ninetieth-birthday visitors invest heavily in presents. Hopefully this will convince my mother that she may carry on for ages. She has to. Otherwise she won't be able to make full use of the new nightie, portable bidet, toiletries and perfumes, eat up all the chocs, or outlast the orchid.

But the Grim Reaper isn't after my mother. He is one for surprises. He is after Rosemary's husband instead. He grabs him suddenly while Rosemary is off having a relaxing swim in the Ladies' Pool.

It is blazing hot. I thought people were meant to die in winter, in January or February when all the fun is over and the freezing cold and drear finishes some of us off, but they all seem to die in summer, when the weather is hot and beautiful and the roses out and it is obvious that they will be missing something pleasant. This is the anniversary of my father's death, and Rosemary's husband collapses and dies four days later. He has had his Last Birthday rather prematurely, at sixty.

Rosemary comes home from her swim to find him on the floor. She feels horribly guilty. There she was, out enjoying herself, and it happened.

The hearse comes to our road. Rosemary and her children want their pictures taken next to it. 'Whatever for?' My mother is astonished. 'I've never heard of that before,' she whispers rather loudly, 'having a photo taken by a hearse.'

Then off they go, and my mother walks behind them. She feels that the hearse will take her bad luck with it. Naturally this all makes her feel very glum and gets her planning again. 'I don't want flowers at my funeral,' she bellows. 'It's a bloody waste of money. They can give it to charity instead.'

She has got me at it. Just in case anyone wants to know, I would like flowers and black horses like Arthur Fowler. If I can't have a horse while I'm alive, then I shall have two when I'm dead. It'll be something to look forward to.

Suitable Clothing

Yesterday I made the mistake of going out in my leggings. There are now certain clothes that I can no longer wear, and when one has a flat, collapsed bottom, very thin legs and gargantuan feet, leggings are in this group. I look very like Max Wall. Nor can I wear short skirts, low necks or tightly fitting garments. Olga also warns me that there is a certain clinging, floppy fabric which I ought to beware of at my age. She spotted salespersons flogging it like mad in some shop in town, lying through their teeth at my peer group.

'You look fabulous Madam. It really suits you,' they cried mendaciously to some under- or overweight ladies swathed in this flobby, soft, knickery material that clung to their every flaw. And the customers believed them. Off they went looking an absolute fright.

Rosemary just saw a woman wearing exactly that material in Venice airport, a pale variety with wishy-washy flowers. 'That was a mistake,' she thought. It was a salutary experience for her. She now plans to give up shorts, even the modest knee-length sort, as she no longer wishes to reveal her giant clumps of varicose veins to the general public.

Yesterday, what I should have done was consult my daughter before leaving the house. If I want a harsh but accurate opinion on my outfits, all I need do is to turn to her, my own in-house image consultant. Much of her life is spent shopping and she is an authority on such things. Only last week she bossed me into

79

buying a pair of bargain trainers in a sale. I personally longed for ordinary plimsolls, but the Daughter insisted, and young persons have been admiring my trainers ever since. They mistake me for someone hip.

Now my mother has spotted the trainers. They are tremendously comfy, especially with her arthritis, and she longs for her own. But she may be stepping onto the road of no return. Once you've got your tracksuit and trainers, and that silvery grey hair, says Olivia, you can say goodbye to life as a sexual being. Perhaps it's the gathering of elastic and thick cotton round the ankles that does it. But my mother is ninety and no longer wishes to be a sexual being, even though it is all the rage now for persons of her age. She is sick of reading about it in magazines and watching it on the telly.

The key clothing word for us seems to be 'flowing'. As leggings are now off the list, jeans give me a stomach-ache and tracksuits make me feel lumpy and look like a capon, loose flowing trousers seem to be the answer, plus flowing skirts and loose tops so that I can drift about with Rosemary looking elegant.

Sometimes, though, on more confident days, one wants to give up the tasteful, flowing stuff and go for something wild. Olga has lent me a rather dashing black velvet strappy number with leopard-pattern frills round the middle. I am off to a party in it. I try to nip past the Daughter but she spots me on the way out.

'Oh my God. What is THAT?'

She is right to be startled. It is short, has a low neck, is tightly fitting and is second-hand. But I love it.

Not So New Man

My friend Fielding is now fifty-one and feeling rather drear. He is balding, riddled with aches and pains, his musculature collapsing, women pay him no attention and he is an embarrassment to his children. This is obviously a difficult time for him. No one enjoys physical decay, but luckily for Fielding, it is less of an impediment to men than to women. If a chap can stay more or less upright for a few minutes, he can still hold a position of tremendous power, like Yeltsin and Deng Xiaoping.

Deng is still alive and functioning, say his daughters. He is ninety-two, often relaxes in front of the telly and has dinner at table with the family. But we last saw him two and a half years ago 'in a wheelchair staring vacantly into space'. This all looks very suspicious to me.

Then Olga reminded me of the legendary El Cid. 'Remember him?' said she briskly. 'He's the one who was tied upright on his horse dead and trotted out at the head of his army to trick the enemy into thinking he was still functioning as a leader.'

This is obviously an ancient tradition – wheeling a chap out dead to lead his country. Reagan, when President, was a more recent example, often seen in a 'rather stiff position', 'standing erect and smiling', or dozing off, with no memory to speak of and Nancy the Iron Twig always right there to hold him up if he toppled. It was El Cid all over again.

Now Mr Yeltsin is doing it. He 'has not been seen since his brief wooden appearance at his inauguration on August 9th', said this newspaper. It's these wooden appearances and vacant stares that give the game away. I must say Mr Yeltsin's thick layer of bronze make-up is a terrific help and inspires confidence, but I think we need to see Deng as well. Just a brief glimpse would do. Why can't he be shunted out briefly like Yeltsin? Facial muscles need not be moved, only the arm and hand, and the legs need to shuffle a few steps. It could all be done by remote control, because technology has improved enormously since El Cid's day.

I don't want to sound sour about all this, but imagine a nearly dead woman in charge. No one would tolerate it for a minute. Only weeks ago I saw three extremely clever elderly women scientists on telly. They could have run the world with their eyes shut, but the most sprightly and brilliant one hasn't even been made a professor.

Still Fielding is not encouraged. 'I've never wanted power,' he drones weedily, 'and I don't like new men. I have no role model. All I'm allowed to do is to be dignified on the road to death.' He plans to lock himself in the spare room and write a novel.

Perhaps I have judged him too harshly. Here he is at a crisis and not even able to blame the menopause. At least he knows his limitations.

New Grandmas

Suddenly the world is teeming with new grandmas. They are my age or younger. Rosemary and I were wandering around the block with the dog when we came across Mrs P, pushing her new baby granddaughter around in a buggy. Baby smiled the most wonderful smile on earth and Rosemary went weak at the knees and had to lean against a lamp-post.

Mrs P was in Heaven. She wants to give up her job as heavy-duty social worker and play with the divine grandchild all day. I have never seen Rosemary look so soppy. She clung to the lamp-post waiting dreamily for the Smile to come again, and this isn't even her grandchild.

My cousin in the North has just had her first charming grandchild, American Cousin has a heavenly granddaughter and Olivia has recently had one. Her grandchild is all the more perfect because she can hand it back to the daughter whenever she wants to go and have a very long bath.

In four months my old friend Jacqueline is to become a grandma too. Friends assure her that having a grandchild is paradise, just like having your own baby over again, but she is just a tiny bit worried about the daughter's capabilities. Although eighteen she is unable to cook or wash up because it ruins her nail varnish. So far all washing and catering has been done by parents, but what happens when she has to plunge her hands into a packet of Pampers, or worse?

And there is another little problem regarding grandchildren.

You cannot choose when you are going to have them. You can't plan. One minute you're a free woman, just about to embark on a new career or thrilling retirement, then along comes the grandchild and exhausted daughter who needs a babysitter once or twice a week, or just for a few days while she works part-time, and if the grandchild also has a divine smile, it's difficult to say no.

But these are all dinky baby grandchildren. Eventually the chubbly, widgy little things may grow into hulking, scowling, chain-smoking adolescents. They may dye their hair yellow, pluck their eyebrows away and pierce their navels, as my daughter has done. My mother has experienced this transformation in her grandchild and still struggles daily to cope with it.

'You used to be such a lovely fat baby,' she moans, staring glumly at her elegant, waif-like granddaughter. 'What happened?'

Naturally the Granddaughter is deeply ashamed, especially if peers are present. 'Shut up Grandma,' says she mortified.

'Don't you tell me to shut up,' roars my mother, top-volume across the double generation gap, and our house is hell again. It is difficult for my mother to cope with this second wave of adolescence. She thought mine was bad enough: the CND, the bare feet, the dismal raggedy clothing, the rock and roll, but nowadays the adolescent is a far more formidable creature, its appearance wilder, its music louder and fiercer, it dances for longer, it takes more drugs, it spends more money and it knows more about sex than ever before. But ours was a divine baby, and she had a heavenly smile. Sometimes she still has.

Looking After Mother

The Community is caring for my friend Anne's mother, but Anne has to help them rather a lot. As she is an artist working at home, she is available at all times of the day and night, to run to Mother's flat when needed, for emergencies, or for things the Community can't do, like taking Mother to the doctor, foot clinic (two-hour wait), diabetic clinic, ear clinic, geriatric consultant.

'I've spent most of the last ten years in Outpatients,' says she, rather quietly.

Life isn't too hot for Mother either, being stuck in a wheelchair with a catheter, diabetic leg ulcers, failing sight and two hip replacements and being almost deaf. Naturally she has grown rather crotchety, often screams with temper and gets through care workers quick as a flash. She's tried Residential Home but been expelled for bad behaviour, so the care workers must keep on coming.

They come in pairs, for one hour morning and evening, to get Mother up, washed, breakfast and lavatory, or undressed, dinner, lavatory and bed. They haven't time for constipation, diarrhoea or broken catheter, so if anything like that happens they summon Anne, three or four times a week, or any other family member if she's not there, or, as last resort, the ambulance. Anne's family is on constant red alert.

We went to visit Mother the other day. She seemed perfectly charming to me, but I didn't have to inject insulin or wipe her bottom or haul her in and out of wheelchairs and cars, take her lunch on Saturdays and have her to stay all Sundays. Visitors perk her up, and I only had to chat briefly and smile nicely.

Then we went home, but Anne hadn't really left her behind. Thoughts of Mother linger in her mind: have I to ring the foot clinic today? Or Doctor, or Social Services? Is the hoist working, are there enough nappies, will the Lodger/Carer come home from work in time to put her to bed/give the vital insulin injection?

Naturally Mother gets nervous as well. Last week, just to check that everything was working as it should in case Anne or the Lodger were ever away, she called the ambulance, police, neighbour and doctor all at once at three a.m. They all turned up together and were furious.

Meanwhile, back at home, Anne's husband is getting on with the secretarial and paper work: filling in forms, fixing up appointments, organising the vast workforce, care workers, OTs, Social Workers, soothing the District Nurse and the GP (who sometimes squabble with the Hospital Consultant and the diabetic clinic) and the carers who get into bates, or run away crying like the last one did. And while they all argue about who does what and how, Mother gets smellier and grumpier.

And now I hear that our charming afternoon visit has back-fired. Mother is convinced that Anne and her husband are secretly plotting to sell her flat and dump her in a loathsome institution, and I am the potential buyer.

What luck that my mother and I haven't got to the bottom-wiping, catheter-changing, paranoid stage yet. Neither of us fancies it. But it could be looming. Here we are, with me freelance and working at home, all ready to go.

Big Sticky-Up Things

As death approaches it is not pleasant for some of us to feel that we are but a tiny speck in the universe and may leave no trace. There are things one can do about this: have children, write a book, or a few poems or recipes, plant a tree. But these modest little reminders are often not enough. Some people like to leave enormous reminders.

I noticed last week that Sir Norman Foster is keen to leave yet another huge sticking-up one. Naturally people have been cracking rude jokes, unable to resist the obvious symbolism, but Sir Norman's longings are nobler than that. He isn't just a small egomaniac desperate to erect an immense, thrusting monument. I suspect that he is, in fact, part of another ancient tradition common among older males.

I realised this while flicking through the tenth-century epic poem *Beowulf* the other day. There was Sir Norman's behaviour replicated to a tee. King Hrothgar designed 'a massive, elaborate and conspicuous monument' to himself. It 'shall stand as a reminder of me,' he droned, 'a house greater than men on earth have ever heard of, towering high above Hronesness' and rearing boldly from a headland. He wasn't the only one. All over the world chaps have been busily erecting huge monuments to themselves. They have tried pyramids, obelisks, monoliths, megaliths, totem poles, skyscrapers, our own Canary Wharf and now the whacking great Petronas Towers.

Blokes are obviously prey to this primitive but irresistible desire. The shape may vary slightly – Hitler and Ceauşescu went for fat, stumpy, brutish ones, Norman's is a long, thin, silvery chic one, but either way, *everyone must notice them for ever*.

It's all this 'rearing, thrusting and bigger than anyone else's' that brings to mind anxieties of a phallic nature, but it can't be that simple. Sir Norman is happy in love and yet he still must build the biggest thing in London. Even his Dr Sex girlfriend cannot curb these desires. So he must be part of the great heroic tradition. It all fits in. Norman is considered a Classicist (compared to Richard Rogers the Romantic) and according to his chums, longs to be 'a heroic figure', just like Hrothgar.

What a pity he is but one of many who, blinded by this heroic tradition, is unaware that people often prefer to live and work on the ground and do not give a fig for obtrusive and gigantic reminders of fellows like Hrothgar, Xerxes, Vat Phu, Emperor This or That, Hitler, Mies, Palumbo and Sir Norman. They probably prefer small reminders of their Mum, Grandpa or favourite Auntie, to be noticed now and again.

Mad on Cooking

My mother is dead keen on cooking. It helps her to relax and has brought her a new role in life – chief chef to the household and teacher of haute cuisine. My friends are flooding round here to attend master classes in the kitchen. They do as they are told, listen carefully and then eat up the thrilling results. Rosemary and Olga are particularly dedicated pupils, forever copying out recipes, obeying orders and oohing and aahing.

'I forget everything else when I'm cooking,' cries my mother cheerily, whirling about the kitchen like a tornado, surrounded by admirers.

I do not attend these lessons. I have never been keen on doing as my mother tells me and somehow cannot start now. I notice that my daughter is following my example to the letter. She will not listen to the tiniest instruction, avoids all domestic tasks, but is highly skilled at microwaving. We are both a disappointment to my mother. What luck that she is encouraged and supported by my friends, and now by the telly, suddenly jam-packed with cookery programmes. She awakes every day to a new one.

'It's Kevin,' she calls happily. 'It's Delia/It's Paul and Jean. Look.' Caught up in the welter of programmes, her table is piled high with scribbled recipes and notepads and we have a thrilling menu – apple tatin, creamed celeriac, chicken with apricots, pear frangipane tart, coulis of this and that.

My mother quotes the words of famous cooks, 'Give me some rocket and balsamic vinegar and I'm anyone's,' she roars. She has made an enormous culture leap – from working-class Barrow-in-Furness via Hove to trendy North London. This is something of an accomplishment at ninety.

Sadly my loathing of cooking never wavers. The more programmes, master classes, demonstrations and discussions, the worse it gets. And now we've found a new fish shop. My mother is in paradise. The fish is heavenly and cheap. It is even better than the fish in Hove. She does bulk buying. We must now be forever talking about the buying and preparation of food, especially fish.

And she has mobilised the neighbourhood. Everyone must collect windfalls, blackberries, green tomatoes and the sour cherries from next door. The fridge and freezer are bursting with pies, purées, chutneys and stewed fruits.

I must admit that on Friday my mother made the best blackberry pie on earth. Then tragedy struck. She could not eat a crumb of it. She was so exhausted and sickened by her huge bout of cooking that she could only lie weak, pale and nauseated in front of the telly sipping fizzy lemonade, a shadow of her kitchen self. It was two days before she could stomach the pie, and by then it had lost its brilliance.

'It's only nice if someone else cooks it,' my mother moaned in a heart-rending way. I agree absolutely. Today we had cheese on toast, made in a flash by me. My mother loved it.

Men in Crisis

Olga has recently discovered, to her surprise, that her two-timing ex-boyfriend was in fact four- or five-timing. Other women are flooding out of the woodwork, some ringing Olga with details and able to compare notes. By careful cross-checking they have pieced together the jigsaw of his movements, exposed his lies and all spurned him en masse.

Rejected and despised by the ex-mistresses, he is hopefully a broken man, but Olga suspects that he has recruited yet another woman from somewhere. And anyway, perhaps we are being rather harsh. This must be a difficult time for him. Greater men have found themselves in a similar position. Look at that bishop the other week, women all over the place, but luckily the Diocese of Oxford has produced two booklets explaining matters. I read them to Olga so she might understand the problem and not take things personally.

'Men in particular,' says the Diocese, 'are more vulnerable to affairs when they pass through critical stages of life.'

'What's so critical?' asks Olga. It's not as if these men were doing badly. One was a bishop, after all, and the boyfriend is a professor, so this must be a crisis age for chaps. Just look at our leaders: 'Shagger' Norris, Alan Clark, Tim Yeo and other famous Ministers seem to have been going quite wild. Here they are, fifty or so, successful, up on a peak or high plateau but not knowing where to go next. Where can they turn except to women?

But the trouble is, even though they're quite grown up, they still don't seem to understand girlies. The Diocese itself, a mentor to some of them, is in a frightful muddle. 'One particularly risky type,' they rave, 'is the female hysterical personality . . . shallow, overly reactive, even vivacious, uninhibited in displaying sexuality, given to romantic fantasy . . . but . . . naive and frigid.'

No wonder a bishop doesn't know what he's heading for when he goes out in the dead of night to counsel a lady parishioner. No wonder his palms are soon sweating and his pulse racing. Obviously Olga's boyfriend had much the same sort of guidance from his public school and Oxford, and so he bumbled out into the world unprepared and made rather a hash of things.

Olga and I are still baffled by these stories from the Diocese. As practising female hysterics we would instinctively avoid a fellow of this age with sweating palms, beating heart and his collar on backwards. Olga swears the Boyfriend's palms were cool as a cucumber. But he did have rather floppy hands and wear a bobble hat, and he is still on the loose. Perhaps she should issue her own new booklet of guidelines.

Bad Teeth Day

What luck that I still have all my teeth. Many of my contemporaries are losing theirs. For months Rosemary has had one top one missing, creating a witch-like gap whenever she takes the false one out. Sometimes she comes for a short dog walk and forgets to replace it. If we need to chat to anyone on our walk, Rosemary must remain mute, cover her mouth or talk sideways. This seems rather unfair. She didn't expect to look like a toothless old hag for at least another couple of decades.

My mother is tormented by her false teeth, but she is ninety. It's my peers that are worrying. Yet another one recently lost his teeth and was unable to taste his dinner at all with his mouth swathed in plastic. He has thrown his false teeth away in a fury, tears at food with his gums and tries not to smile at people.

And now the dentist has wrenched out Rosemary's remaining front ones without anaesthetic. I find her whimpering and traumatised with her hand over her mouth. Her family seems to be suffering the mishaps of old age prematurely. Her poor sister is whizzed into Hospital for a heart operation (the one with the blow-up balloon that Yeltsin couldn't have), just on Rosemary's bad teeth day.

More bad luck: the Hospital is full, no beds, the operation postponed. 'Come back at two o'clock,' says the Hospital. Postponed again. 'Come back at five-thirty.' Back and forth drive toothless Rosemary and her breathless sister, until at last she is admitted. But the operation fails. It must be done again in the morning. Luckily Rosemary has the new teeth whacked in before her next visit to Hospital.

Sister is in intensive care all day, checked every half-hour. Next day she may go home, all the way to Hertfordshire. 'Don't forget,' says the Hospital cheerily, 'for the next forty-eight hours you are still our patient.' This will be difficult from forty miles away. Half-an-hour later, when Rosemary collects the sister's tablets, there is a new patient already installed in her bed. Hospital is shunting the heart patients through in a flash now that they have the hang of this new mini-balloon treatment.

No wonder they are full up if we all start cracking up at fifty. Rather more of my contemporaries than I would like have been desperately poorly recently. I often wake in the night convinced it is my turn next. Luckily the sister recovers and Rosemary looks charming with her sparkly new teeth in. She is giving up smoking and I am scrubbing and flossing my teeth on the hour. We have a reprieve. But for how long?

Sandwich Generation

My friend Anne is in a tricky position. She is stuck between two rather confusing generations: the teenage son in her home and the very elderly mother up the road. Which one is a grown-up? She can never tell. Both need dinners and attention. The mother has nappies and tantrums, the son still needs food supplies and supervision. To his mind he is a grown-up but still needs assistance, especially with the mass catering, laundry and bed and breakfast facilities when his friends come to visit.

What luck that her mother lives up the road. In our house my mother and daughter are crammed into the same premises. A teenager is a difficult creature to understand, especially from two generations away, so naturally things have been rather tense here, what with three generations of problems. Exams and romance, finance and household drudgery, arthritis and angina have all taken their toll and our home is now a tinderbox.

We desperately need a holiday each, but how? Easy enough for my daughter, free as a bird. She is off to Greece, but my mother's requirements are more complex: no stairs, charming company, full-time attendant, high-quality cuisine and fresh air.

Luckily she is able to escape on a mini-holiday and so am I. She visits Ruislip, my childhood home, where my very old friend Jacqueline has her to stay. What a friend! She attends to my mother's every need for five days and provides visitors, delightful garden, home-grown produce and constant chat. My mother has a tremendous holiday. Five days without the rows, shrieking, vile language, tantrums, dribbling barking dog, streams of teenage visitors and layers of mess that make life in our house a hell on earth. Meanwhile I am off for three days to the country with the dog. Bliss.

No wonder my mother looks tremendously well upon my return, her complexion glowing, her ankles slim, her mood light-hearted and optimistic. But once she is back in town her decline is rapid. The ankles swell, her strength and vitality go, and she retreats glumly to her bedroom. As night falls, troops of large and hulking visitors tramp past her door on the way to Granddaughter's room to do God knows what. My mother cannot rest. She knows that cigarettes are being smoked, the larder is emptying, the debris piling up and her grandchild hurtling down the road to ruin.

But all is not drear. Sometimes things lighten up in our house. One day Granddaughter behaves perfectly. She tidies, she washes up, she makes tea, she does homework, she bans visitors. But my mother cannot adapt to this sudden change. She cannot praise her grandchild. 'About bloody time too,' she snaps, stamping into the garden.

Naturally my daughter is disappointed. 'Why is Grandma always horrid to me?' she cries and runs weeping to her room. My mother grumps about the garden, my daughter sobs upstairs. I find that on these occasions I tend to play football with the dog. Which is the grown-up in our house?

The End Is Nigh

This is a nerve-racking time to be old and helpless, what with the NHS being in crisis. 'Non-urgent cases' are told to wait for their operations for months at home, sometimes in chronic pain, or are abandoned by Casualty for hours on trolleys in badly lit public corridors. Now in Hillingdon the Over-Seventy-fives may not go to hospital at all. Even nursing homes are fairly dicey. Luckily we found a place for my Auntie, the only home that smelled fragrant, but other poor old aunties are not so lucky They could easily get compulsory day-time telly, the odd slap round the face, or even a quick scald in the bath.

Only the other day I was remembering my father's last stay in hospital. It was not pleasant. As there are so many elderly patients and so few nurses, it is something of a toss-up as to whether you get turned, moved, changed or fed enough. Or whether your drip gets filled and your scan done. My father's didn't and wasn't.

'How was my father the day before he died?' I asked the Consultant, 'You saw him.'

'Quite frankly I can't remember,' said the Consultant in something of a bate. 'I do have four hundred patients in four hospitals.' Perhaps my father would have done better in Hillingdon, forced to stay at home, where we would have remembered who he was.

If only Dr Swift was still around to dash off another relevant Modest Proposal, for the consumption of the English elderly this time rather than Irish babies. But what can one do with the elderly? The situation is even worse. They are no longer plump and juicy and so unfit for a ragout or fricassée. Biltong would be the only option, but it is not much in demand. Or perhaps mass cryogenics is the answer. Then when we've worked out how to make everybody twenty-one again, attractive and useful, they can all be defrosted and recalled.

But these are barbaric and costly proposals. Voluntary euthanasia seems to be the only way forward. It is a low-cost, do-it-yourself solution, and we have after all reached the end of the road. Time to face up to things. The country just has no more money to spare – not after years and years of the young, energetic and greedy being encouraged to plunder the economy at the expense of the old, frail and considerate. At least our Queen is now travelling by public transport. She is perhaps saving up for a hip-replacement.

Garden Centre Rage

My friend Sylvia has managed to turn old age to her advantage, briefly. There she was, trying to get into the garden centre car park, but the way was blocked by a foolish fellow who had parked his car in the entrance.

The young woman in front of Sylvia confronted this chap in a fury. She threatened to call the police, she jumped up and down screaming with temper, but still the pillock refused to budge.

Then Sylvia had a try. Cleverly she crawled out of her car in a pathetic, stooping way (she is a skilled actress), tottered up to him and spoke.

'You see,' she explained, just like a silly old woman (she is seventy-four), 'we can't move if you stay here, and there are lots of cars behind us.' Then, although she would have preferred to punch him in the chops, she smiled nicely and said please.

The dullard snarled and agreed to move and everyone was able to enter the car park. 'I'm still furious,' screamed the young woman, bursting with temper. 'The stupid *!!* *!*!*.'

'It's no good,' said Sylvia, 'you must keep calm and do yogic breathing.'

She was thrilled with her performance, an unprecedented success. She and I have often tried telling silly people what to do on our dog walks. We've tried being polite, we've tried shrieking. It gets us nowhere, but there is nothing like having a scream at someone annoying in open countryside to get rid of urban stress.

How did Sylvia manage to control herself this time? Why did the man obey her? 'I was not a threat to him,' she explained. 'This other young woman was rather attractive. He felt threatened.'

But perhaps she is wrong. It is easier to be Mrs Nice if someone else is being Mrs Nasty. And Rosemary suspects that people are nervous of the elderly and infirm. Last Christmas, long before she had her sparkly new false teeth, she'd been out for festive drinks and noticed the police ahead, stopping all drivers to weed out seasonal drunks, so she cunningly took out her false tooth, leaving an unsightly gap, and when the young policeman stopped her, coyly held her hand over her mouth.

'I'm a bit embarrassed,' she mumbled into her hand (blocking any fumes of alcohol), 'but I'm having a bit of trouble with my teeth.'

The policeman went red and waved her off, backing away as if repelled by her decrepitude. Rosemary was tremendously relieved. She was deeply ashamed of her misdeed, but we now know that to avoid confrontation or trouble, merely stoop, dribble or take your teeth out.

HRT

I am finding life rather gruelling. My legs ache, my mother is poorly, I have a teenage daughter and I am bad-tempered. Apparently I am not alone. Dreadful things often happen to women of my age: our parents become ill and die, our children grow up and play up, husbands or partners may disappear and awful things can go wrong with one's body.

We live on a knife-edge. Rosemary's throat now closes up in her sleep. She must go to bed in a somewhat unbecoming mask attached to a tube and air supply, looking rather like the Elephant Man. No wonder some of us become foul-tempered and depressed and are tempted by HRT. But I cannot make my mind up.

My friend X had a grim time on it a couple of years ago. Her adolescent daughter had plunged into a life of sex and drugs, her mother died, she lost her job, her sex life went down the pan. So she wept at the doctor, who whacked her on to HRT. No blood test, no check-up. She describes it rather bitterly. Awfully good for depression, the complexion, the hair, osteoporosis, lack of interest in sex, hot flushes, recurrent cystitis, bad temper, problems with body fluids, sinus, cross-eyes and big ears, says she. It's Prozac for girls.

You can have red pills, blue pills, yellow pills, pairs of brown pills, patches, injections, implants, smear-ons, for short-term, long-term or ever. It seemed a bit of a lucky dip but my friend took it anyway. She was rewarded thirty days later by a grinding backache and seven-day niagara of blood. She rang the doctor in a fright.

'Quite normal,' said the doctor. 'Carry on.'

She carried on. Naively she went off on holiday somewhere hot. Back came the niagara, her face swelled up, her eyes disappeared, squidged up beneath the fat, she felt like hell and threw the HRT away. Her daughter was still a nightmare, her mother still dead and she remained unemployed.

This story rather puts me off, but I hear that HRT is magic for some women. Their skin and hair look gorgeous, they feel like heaven, they become even-tempered sex goddesses once more, and look at Theresa Gorman – a model to us all.

Tempted by the possibility of divine sex and a sunny personality, Olga started it a few months ago. Her doctor was ever so cautious, but Olga begged and stamped her foot until she got it. Before HRT she was tired of life and scarcely able to tie up her shoelaces. But now the Two Possibilities have come true.

Perhaps I should be off to the doctor.

Old Girls

Last week I went to an Old Girls' reunion party. There were all these grown-up women that I hadn't seen for thirty-eight years, luckily all labelled. You look at the label, then at the woman's face, and out of the mist floats an old picture of the schoolgirl: the one who had terrible hay-fever, the one who knew all about boys, the tall shy one and the one who wore ever such smart underwear.

This party was held in a charming, spacious and immaculately tidy rectory, a far cry from my own cramped slum. Naturally I expected only smart and sensible grown-ups. What a relief to find two broken marriages at my table. I am not the only girl to have grown up and made a hash of things. Here was a mixture of success and disaster – errant husbands, sulky disappearing children, stepchildren, new husbands, hip-replacements and luckily, just opposite me, a lady who had retired to the country and turned to dogs. This is my ambition. It is not often that one has the chance to drone on about dogs at table and gaze at photos of squidgy puppies.

Naturally this woman is regarded as batty in her village, just as I am in my street. How come we never discovered this affinity at school and became chums? But we hardly noticed each other then. I used to play with three other girls, and there is one of them. Her news is most extraordinary. All three of them married the chaps they met at sixteen and are still with these fellows thirty-eight years later, and happy. What a staggering achievement for nowadays!

And someone remembers my mother, sweeping from the medical room in a fury after the doctor had criticised my weight. Was I being adequately fed?

This must have been a bitter and humiliating experience for my mother, whose life was spent ensuring that I swallowed as much lovely food as possible. But however much I ate, my twig legs and arms would grow no fatter. So she left the medical room, a strikingly glamorous figure, shouting, 'She throws chicken about at home.'

My school friend has never forgotten it. What could my mother have meant? And did I remember, asked the Dog Lady, 'making up lists of very rude words, then looking them up in the dictionary?' She alone, of all the girls with rude lists, was caught by the sewing mistress. What a moving story! But perhaps we didn't do too badly.

'It appears that none of us have died,' said she later over the phone. 'Among eighty women aged fifty-four someone easily could have.'

Perhaps our school was good for us after all.

Fifteen Wasted Years

This week I heard from another old friend with whom I had fallen out fifteen years ago. It was his sixtieth birthday. I had thought he was cross with me and he thought I was cross with him. We were both wrong, so there were fifteen years wasted. What a dreadful shame. We now had to catch up on all the missing news.

'And how is So-and-so?' he asks. 'You know, that blonde girl who worked for you-know-who.'

'Can't remember,' I say, 'but what about that man, what's his name, with the friend, you know?'

We had a bit of a problem piecing everything together. My friend has had trouble with his memory. 'So bad I had to go to hospital about it,' says he.

'What happened in the hospital? I think he told me but I can't remember. We remembered bits and names, and then they slipped away. By the end of a sentence, the name had gone.

This was a relief to me. Only recently Rosemary criticised my loss of memory as if it were a unique and ghastly failing. I was just telling her a gripping little story when she stopped dead in her tracks and glared as if at a raving lunatic.

'You told me that yesterday,' said she, with staring eyes and gaping jaw. 'And last week you told Mrs X the same thing two days running. You *must* do something about this,' said Rosemary strictly. '*It is serious.*'

'That's the trouble when you speak to a lot of people,' I explained. 'You think not that you repeated something, but that you mentioned it to someone different last time. Or you may specially not tell somebody something because you thought you'd already told them, but in fact you'd told somebody else, and now this person is furious because you've failed to tell them what everyone else knows.'

Then Rosemary told me something she'd already droned on about last night. Naturally I criticised harshly, but Rosemary insisted that *her* repetition didn't count because she had preceded it with 'I know I may have mentioned this already but . . .'

What a cheap trick! Anyone can pretend that they think they may be repeating themselves. Later I rang my old friend back. What a pleasant change not to have one's memory criticised.

'You know that story about the man with the apple that you thought I told you?' said he. 'Well, the way I remember, it was *you* that told *me*.' He was right. Now I remember. For fifteen years I have been telling people a fairy story about the Apple Man.

But which people?

Uneasy Rider

Bad news from my friend in the North. Her horse is not pregnant. It has had awfully bad wind instead. This has been a nerve-racking time for my friend, forced to spend much of the last few months with her head between the horse's legs or under its tail examining the relevant bits. This added to her anxiety. What if passers-by were to regard her with suspicion?

But at last she can go riding again. Naturally the horse is rather wild. It has, after all, been confined for ages pretending to be pregnant and now, free to gallop about, it is forever bolting and rearing. This is tough on my friend at her age after weeks of relative inactivity. She is in constant pain and cannot cross her legs without lifting one up manually and hauling it over the other.

Still she rides on. What a brave woman. I tried riding recently after a gap of twenty years. It is the only time I have longed for a fat bottom. Bouncing up and down for three hours on an ageing thin one was rather gruelling. How does my friend manage?

'You just go through the pain barrier,' says she robustly, 'then it's all right.' And riding has done her no end of good. After a year of it she can now cut her toenails with ease. Before that it had been an enormous struggle – one foot up on a chair, reading lamp and glasses on. But now she can swing her leg straight up onto the table. She's lost a stone in weight, regained her youthful figure and can eat like a pig.

But if, stuck in town like me, you cannot thunder about on a horse, then you can at least exercise the brain. Apparently it improves with exercise. Give an elderly rat a new toy and its brain cells may branch out, connect up and make the rat cleverer. Same with an elderly woman. Just learn a musical instrument or play bridge and the brain will sprout synapses all over the place, so I am told.

And there are things one can do with even less effort. While out dog-walking this morning Sylvia and I met a woman of seventy-three whom Sylvia knew vaguely.

'I've just got married again,' the woman called out through the biting wind.

'Congratulations,' we yelled back. 'Lucky you. What a bold move.'

'It's difficult at this age,' she roared, 'but I couldn't stand being alone.'

I was very impressed but Sylvia wasn't. Perhaps she is right. I shall give marriage a miss but plod on with the cello and book a riding holiday instead. No wonder headmistresses nationwide are clamouring for early retirement. Look at the things one can start doing at fifty-plus. The choices are endless.

Age Rage

The world is growing more annoying by the minute. Only yesterday I rang the building society and was spoken to by a pretend machine woman telling me which button to choose, then a real woman who couldn't answer my question, then another woman who knew nothing, then another machine woman, then another woman who spoke as if advertising cream cheese. Naturally I had a shout. I often have a shout. people blame the menopause, but I blame technology.

This morning I screamed loudly at the dustbin men blocking the road with their cart. They were thrilled. They had tried hard to enrage the queue of motorists behind them by dawdling, smirking and carefully parking in the narrowest bits of road, and now at last they had succeeded. A silly woman had lost her temper. Had I been on a tractor behind a herd of cows I should have been calm as anything, but sitting in a machine and blocked by a machine, I flew into a temper.

There is nothing like a middle-aged woman in a temper to get people crying out 'Menopause' in a mocking way. Never mind if the woman is trapped by slowcoach, sneering men, machines that will not function, hordes of telephonists who can answer no questions, complex and temperamental machinery and queues of traffic. Obviously I would hate to sound bitter, but should a man leap out of a car and stab someone to death just because he looked a trifle annoying, no one would smirk and mutter 'Mid-life-crisis'.

At last I escaped the car and rushed to meet Sylvia on the Heath. There she was, in a pleasant mood in the winter sunshine and breathing properly. I told her my horrid story. The beauty of the Heath escaped me. Sylvia had to point out the golden leaves, glittering frost and clear blue sky. And it was her birthday – seventy-six. What a ghastly start to her day to meet a chum who was breathless, red-faced and apoplectic from screaming. I am deeply ashamed. Sylvia was unruffled.

But next week she may be, however carefully she breathes. She is flying to Madrid with a chum for a short holiday. Already her nerves are in shreds. Large aeroplanes are plummeting from the skies, Madrid is having its highest rainfall for two hundred years, she cannot wear boots because of her bunion, and the banks seems unable to acquire any pesetas. Three times they have promised some, three times Sylvia has trudged there, and all for nothing. If they aren't there next time, she too may have a shout. What luck that Sylvia is seventy-six. It can't possibly be the menopause.

Observers may even have to sympathise.

Birthdays

Olga's birthday is just before Christmas. What bad luck. One lot of presents instead of two. And she doesn't even get what she wants. In her line of work she can't afford to splash out on frivolous luxuries, so she wants to be showered with them on her birthday. No one will do this. Just because she's a left-wing artist people struggle year after year to buy her meaningful presents. She now has a shelf of unintelligible but worthy books when all she really longs for are glamorous soaps, bubble-baths, chocs and flowers.

At least Olga is fairly cheerful about her birthday. Rosemary shudders at the word birthday and cannot articulate a response, and Olivia always cries on hers. If left alone for a moment she will start to blub. She feels not just alone in her kitchen but alone in the whole world.

A few weeks ago I was fifty-four. It threw my mother into a panic. 'You are forty-nine,' she bellowed, 'and from now on you're to go backwards.' To distract us all I organised a welter of parties. Rushing about planning, cooking, celebrating and drinking heavily, one is inclined to forget that the grave is beckoning from just a little nearer than it was last year.

And with any luck a birthday can go on for weeks, especially if one's family tend to squabble. I need one birthday outing with my daughter, one tea-party at home for my mother, one out with close friends and one big one so that the people who annoy each other will be able to talk to someone else.

'You always do this,' says my American cousin. 'You do it year after year. It goes on and on like a Polish wedding.'

She tries to ignore hers. The older she gets the more quickly the birthdays seem to whiz by. She barely gets over one and then along comes the next one.

But there is a solution. We can do each other's birthdays. Olivia can do Olga's, I do my mother's, the Lodger and Rosemary do mine, and Rosemary's children and I do hers. This is paradise for the person doing the birthday. Not only do they feel lovely and kind, but it is not *their* birthday. Perhaps this is what birthdays are for, to make other people happy. Secretly it is the dog's birthday's that bothers me most. When no one is looking I give it a special chicken dinner with banana for pudding. This party is over in two minutes. I try not to cry. The dog is nine and may only have a couple of birthdays left. Luckily it doesn't know.

Old Cynics

Our government seems to be in disarray. Perhaps they will be toppled at last, but I am not excited. It is difficult, as one gets older, not to feel pessimistic about the future. What is the point of complaining, demonstrating or voting in order to try and improve the world? By this age we know perfectly well that Britain is run by the City, the Third World is run for the benefit of the First World, and the rest run by very rich men, gangsters or crazed fundamentalists. What good is one weedy little vote for Labour in North London?

Anyway, it's a safe Labour seat here. It won't make any difference. At least that's what Olga and I thought until last week. Then she went off to a ward meeting with an old friend who still battles on hopefully. There were others there from an older generation who still refused to give up hope, but they are the old school, trained to keep going by their youthful experiences in Communist Party cells. They still trundle out on misty nights to attend ward meetings, while we, the new elderly, often don't bother.

Olga felt rather guilty after this meeting, all the more so because she hadn't bothered to take her purse, such is her apathy, and so couldn't buy raffle tickets. The stalwarts must have thought this a rather lame excuse, but at least she is now reinspired and planning to vote.

Perhaps I should follow her example. The bulk of elderly pessimists seem to be on the left, which has perhaps brought about its downfall. On the right, meanwhile, people vote obediently until death. They do not question policies, nor feebly abstain or have soppy idealists on their side.

Feeling rather hopeless last month I mentioned to the Daughter and her friend that I might vote Green. 'No,' cried the friend strictly. 'It's a wasted vote.' She dresses almost entirely in pink and her home is a shrine to Barbie and Cindy, so this remark was rather unexpected. And she lives in a squat. This brings back my youth – marching all the way from Aldermaston, canvassing, sitting down in roads and rioting in squares. How inspiring. Obviously we must press on, otherwise it will all have been a waste of time.

For the last election we held a party at our house, a dismal experience. By three a.m. everyone had gone to bed in despair except for one guest who sat weeping in front of the telly. One can never be sure of success. Dare we risk another party this time?

Andropause

There is a name for the male menopause – the andropause. Why is it not bandied about here? My friend from Italy tells me that chaps over there, being more relaxed about their bodies, chatter freely about such things – hormonal changes, mood swings, bodily functions, unlike the frozen British male, says she, who cannot abide such talk.

So perhaps it is time to confront the male menopause head on. It seems to be even more of a problem than the menopause. With the menopause one need only sit dumpily at home or have the odd shout, but a last burst of testosterone can cause uproar. It is difficult not to notice. For weeks the news has been bunged up with older men doing grand, pointless, dangerous and very expensive things.

Fiennes has gone trudging off into the Arctic wasteland, Branson has gone up in his silly balloon, Bullimore has got stuck in his yacht a thousand miles from anywhere, Brian Blessed has been crawling up mountains, and as often as not they fail and have to be rescued at vast expense. They are rewarded by piles, kidney-stones, trenchfoot, stump-fingers and frostbite. But perhaps they are helpless in the grip of the Change.

Even so, there are cheaper options. If one really needs to be brave and suffer intense pain and discomfort, then it can be done absolutely free on the Heath. People do it here day after day in a modest way with hardly a word to anyone. Only last week I was staggering about out there with the dog, the wind biting my face off, when I met Mrs X returning from her swim in the open-air Ladies' Pool. She is seventy-plus, the attendants had to break the ice for her, but still she goes twice a day. What's more she is the picture of health.

Apparently this is the most exhilarating thing in the world, and the trick with winter swimming is to keep on doing it. (That way you avoid a heart attack.) And most of the female winter swimmers are over sixty. What tremendous bravery – *and* inexpensive and harmless.

Meanwhile Kathy, the cleaning lady, cannot get rid of her brother. For days now he has been glued to her couch watching telly. This andropause obviously takes a variety of forms. He is fifty, unemployed and divorced and will not go home, but sits depressed and inert, blighting her home. If only he would spring up, help with the washing up and chatter about his problems like those Italians, but no such luck.

'He just sits there using up my electricity,' says Kathy. In his own small way he is causing havoc and bankruptcy. If only he would go off in a balloon.

Bad Knicker Day

Yesterday I put my knickers on sideways without realising. What is going on? I put one leg through a leg, the other through the waist and my body through the other leg. I only discovered this in the late afternoon when stepping into my bath. Later I nipped round to see Rosemary, hoping that she would be slopping around in her carpet slippers and droodgy cardigan, but no such luck. Her daughter had bought her a chic, dark blue Chenille number for Xmas and she looked extremely dashing. What's more, she has thrown away her grunty old slippers and is dynamically planning her retirement. She has found a heavenly cottage down in Cornwall and wants to move and live there forever. Her whole life is planned out and I am still struggling with my knickers.

'You must be very thin,' said Rosemary strictly, 'or your knickers are very out of shape.'

But she is wrong. They are not out of shape. They are just the new style. And the weather is partly to blame. On a dark and freezing morning one hardly wants to be studying the day's knickers for ages before putting them on, and modern knickers are more difficult to work out. The high-cut leg makes waist and leg exits the same width.

Looking at them once they are on the body is even more depressing. For anyone with even a slightly saggy bottom, they are very cruel garments. For anyone with a pear-shaped bottom, they are a disaster. This style has wrecked the summers for me.

All bikinis are now cut in this unfortunate way, making the thighs look like an uncooked side of ham.

Once, a few years ago, swept away by the glamour of the place, I bought a high-cut, leopardskin bikini in Milan. I looked rather chic in the shop, but once out on the beach, by the pool or even in the garden, the enormous white thighs were thrown into relief. A ruthless new bikini-line was attended to, but even then the Daughter was horrified and obliged to sit several yards away from me in public.

So all in all I find the shape of modern knickers distressing. First they disappear at the side, then the whole back goes missing and only a central string remains. Only people with utterly perfect bottoms may wear them, and I hear that leotards have gone the same way. So I am off to the old ladies' department for a proper pair, a winceyette nightie and thermal vests for me and my mother. In winter, we are the lucky ones.

To Coldly Go

The cold is turning my mother into a slug-a-bed. She has not left the house for days and lies endlessly watching telly. Last week I found her gripped by a programme on euthanasia.

'Would you do that for me?' she asked glumly.

I told her I might have to go to prison for murder but she was unmoved. She is not the only one. My friend Sylvia is also fed up with the weather. She hasn't looked upwards for weeks. Why bother? She is sick of looking at the endless grey. We had a short euthanasia debate on our dog-walk. Sylvia too has been contemplating death and has written a Living Will. And if the doctors here refuse to do as they're told, then she'll be off to Holland.

'I have lots of friends there,' says she, 'and it's much nearer than Australia.'

'Will the friends be lined up with their cushions?'

Sylvia won't say, but she is determined. My mother is cheered to think that she is not the only one contemplating suicide. She changes her mind and makes some fishcakes instead.

Just in case she sinks into another gloom, I force her to get up next day and attend her Bridge Club. Bridge is a dangerous game that she plays every Wednesday. The room is hot, the noise deafening and every table packed with players prey to outbursts of temper, bad behaviour and rudeness that would never be tolerated elsewhere. The room simmers with repressed loathing. Often the loathing bursts out.

'I'm not playing with that horrible man,' shouted my mother last week. 'I come here to RELAX.' By tea-time her nerves were in shreds. I arrived to find her on the brink of a fight. She had been guarding her friend's seat in the tea-room when along came another old lady and sat in it without so much as a by-your-leave.

'Do you mind!' roared my mother. 'This is my friend's chair and I'm saving it.'

'Well, it's my chair now,' said the Rude Lady, and just in the nick of time, back came the friend and elbowed/Zimmer-framed the interloper out of the way.

'Bloody old COW,' said my mother, in what she thought was an undertone, but the Lady whipped round in a fury.

'What did you say?' she snapped fiercely. The tea-room fell silent. Would there be bloodshed?

'I said "I don't want a ROW",' lied my mother cleverly, emphasising the rhyming word, off lumbered the deposed woman and along came the tea and cake trolley. My mother couldn't wait to get back to bed and the telly. It is, she now realises, a delightful option.

Three Mothers

Rosemary tells me that three of her friends have come up with a gem of an idea for their elderly mothers. They have bought a rambling property out in Norfolk and are about to install the mothers in it. Social Services are thrilled. Three of their clients, formerly scattered all over the county, can now all be visited in one swoop.

For now the daughters will all visit the mothers in shifts, but they have cleverly applied for early retirement. Then they will all move into the rambling property, the ancient mothers will eventually fade out and the three friends take their places, grow old and live happily together to the end. But first of all they are going to train the mothers to play bridge, eat pleasantly together at table and like each other.

Ha ha. Some hopes. Rosemary and I have tried to make our mothers be friends but they will not oblige. It is bad enough forcing your child to play with your friends' children, never mind making your mothers chum up. Olga and I tried to combine our children when they were teeny. They whacked each other with robots, fought over the Wendy house and grew up to regard each other with disdain.

Meanwhile my mother is the most rebellious. She was horrified to find that Rosemary's mother is frittering her money on herself, rather than handing it over to her struggling widowed daughter. Here is my mother scrimping and saving it all for me, and there is Rosemary's mother relaxing on holiday in San

Francisco while Rosemary slaves away in the Inner City. My mother is horrified. She now finds fault with Rosemary's mother's every word, action, movement or breath.

'What do I want a letter from *her* for,' shouts my mother in a fury. 'Why do I want to know what *she's* doing?' Rosemary's mother kindly sends cards and regards to my mother, and this is the response she gets. We keep my mother's behaviour a secret. Imagine the two of them banged up together in Norfolk.

Perhaps the other three mothers could be placed in perimeter cottages while the daughters share the central mansion. But perhaps our own mothers are just not a good match. Mine is bold, forthright and rarely quiet, Rosemary's is a polite Christian. Other mothers may be better behaved.

Meanwhile Rosemary's mother rather envies mine. If my mother can live with me, why can't she live with Rosemary? My mother has described the hell on earth that is living with one's daughter, but Rosemary's mother cannot believe it. This envy could easily turn to loathing. We shall not be searching for a large property in the country.

Meetings Can Be Deadly

Rosemary was stuck in a very dull staff meeting the other day. On and on it went, with members of staff droning in the sort of modern phraseology that Rosemary abhors, about 'interfacing, planning modules, monitoring and evaluating, gender issues' and 'reflective practice', until she was ready to scream and shout.

Then suddenly she was saved by a thrilling fantasy in which she placed all staff in their coffins ready for burial. As the meeting progressed, more and more of them were laid out. Listening to one staggeringly dull fellow, she dreamed to herself, 'One more boring remark and you're dead.' Naturally he made one, so Rosemary placed him in a coffin and planned his funeral service. Would everyone be singing drear hymns, or reciting a dull sociology text? Would there be flowers? How many cars? Would a secret mistress lurk behind a tree in the cemetery?

She later told some chums about her fantasy. This is apparently a common academic pastime, they said, except that most people plan orgies instead of burials. Olga agrees. She tends to place people in bed with their wives, if she knows the wives. If not, she makes up a suitable wife, or partner, occasionally pairing up two colleagues, but never more than two. Then she imagines the proceedings. Staff meetings just fly by. She has perfected a method of nodding and saying 'Yes' in an understanding way, just as if she had grasped every nuance of the meeting.

I remember doing the very same in the staff room of a comprehensive school. With such a large staff, possibilities were infinite, and what a good job that I paid no attention to the National Curriculum. The vast tracts of it that I might have laboured over have now been deleted anyway.

'Take out pages 39 to 83,' instructed one visiting Curriculum adviser. We all did. 'Now throw it away.' What bad luck for those who had read it carefully.

When I was younger and had the strength, I tried to read the Curriculum and came across a sentence 71 words long. It contained not a single comma. The meaning of it eluded me. So I thought of other more thrilling things, but not burials. Now that I am older and nearer to death than sex, I see that Rosemary's dream would have been more fitting. Who wrote that 71-word sentence? Who wrote the reams of mystifying crapolata that millions of teachers sweated over for hours, days and weekends, and all for nothing? Rosemary's fantasy is just the one for them.

Harsh New World

A terrible sense of emptiness hit me the other day. There is not a single costume drama left on telly. Over the last year I have come to rely on them – the period frocks, the bonnets, horses, carriages and country houses, charming manners, witty chat, repressed sex and happy endings. I need at least one hour of it on Sundays to get me through the week.

Perhaps I am wallowing in the past because the present and future look rather bleak. Rosemary and I realised the other day that we are lucky to be over fifty and shall be dead before things get much worse.

As we walked the dog round the block the other night we noticed that many windows on the top floors of the houses were open, despite the bitter weather, and teenagers were hanging out of them puffing various sorts of smoke into the freezing night air and wasting the central heating. Rosemary and I suspected marijuana.

Apparently the children are under great stress nowadays and no wonder. The world is going down the drain and they must go with it. Here we are plagued by Third World debt, pollution, corruption, festering mountains of nuclear waste, rampaging new diseases, poisoned hamburgers and Andrew Lloyd Webber musicals. No wonder today's youth seem rather wild.

And our house is alive with teenagers. This is hell for my mother, especially at weekends when the Daughter's chums stream through the house, clomping up and down the stairs past her bedroom. She sees the long or matted hair, the skateboards, the raggedy clothes, hears the noise, foul language and thumping music and smells the ciggy smoke, and naturally it sets her shouting.

'Who the bloody hell is that?' she roars. 'No smoking in this house.' The youths tiptoe up and down, my mother shoots out of her room like the Troll under the Billy Goats' bridge, defending our home. To her they are not some other mothers' babies in a stressful world, but big strange men, many of whom clump downstairs again and use her lavatory. If there's anything my mother cannot bear, it is a strange man's bottom on her lavatory. And she has taken to hiding the candelabra. What if a youth should spot it gleaming in her bedroom and make off with it? She lives on a knife-edge.

Who can blame her? The young are a strange lot. Things were much pleasanter in our day. We went to bed earlier, did more homework, knew our tables, had better pop songs, better clothes and less dangerous habits. Soon we shall be the stuff of costume dramas.

Take My Rings

The winter solstice, the cold snap and the freezing fog have passed and my mother is still here. She is most surprised. Only weeks ago the angina struck and she was prepared for the worst.

'Take my rings,' cried my mother movingly. 'Hide them. I'm not going into hospital with them on. Take them now or you'll forget.' She held up her hands weakly. I took the rings off and hid them in a drawer, feeling rather like a robber.

I think my friend Olivia may have saved her life. At the beginning of winter my mother's room was an icebox. It has two exterior walls facing north and east and reminded her of the frozen steppes of her homeland. Friends and relatives were shocked that I allowed my elderly mother to live in a refrigerator, but luckily Olivia came up with a plan.

The two iced walls had to be curtained. We were to go to Brent Cross Shopping Centre to buy ready-made curtains. It sounds a simple plan – buy curtains. Really it meant measure everything, buy curtain linings, curtain rods, hooks, bedcovers to match the curtains, cushions to enhance the bed, covers for the cushions and hundreds of complex calculations.

This was a grim outing for someone like me – an elderly and short-tempered woman who has tried from her earliest youth to avoid any type of shopping. There I was shuffling, standing and fiddling around, legs aching, numerous difficult choices and decisions to be made and not a single chair in sight. After ten minutes I was desperate to lie down and scream. Hopefully four hours in Brent Cross guarantees my mother's eternal admiration and a place in heaven for Olivia and me.

Luckily Olivia had her tape-measure and notebook ready. For hours she stood measuring and counting, wandered about choosing and matching, stopped for a tea-break, continued choosing, and four hours later we had everything, and a new convector heater.

At last it was over. Just a few more days of fitting, altering, and sewing for Olivia and my mother's premises were transformed. She is now surrounded by acres of turquoise curtain, delightfully patterned cushions and matching bedspread. Her room is a boiler-house.

My mother staggers from it fanning herself. 'It looks like a tart's boudoir,' says she, thrilled to bits. The glamorous curtains have perked her up no end. She has asked for her rings back, a snowdrop has appeared on the lawn, the almond blossom is coming out and she is now on the lookout for sticky buds again. It is almost time for my mother's fifth Last Spring.

Ruder and Ruder

Fielding has been reading his teenage daughter's magazines. They are shocking. It's not just the content but also the attitude that upsets him. A girl is advised to make tremendous demands on her boyfriend nowadays. He must be a sensitive and wildly adventurous lover, doing the sort of things that still turn Fielding slightly queasy.

'In my day you just showed up, said hallo, got it over with and then went down the football,' says he sulkily. 'Now you have to *relate* to them.' Other blokes can do it. Fielding has watched them at it. They talk earnestly to women, listen in a caring way to their problems, about how stressful life is, how hard they work, what insensitive pigs their boyfriends are, give the girls a Kleenex and hey presto, they're in.

No wonder Fielding still hasn't a clue. In his teens he read *Eagle* and the *Children's Newspaper*, which told him how to oil his Hornby-OO. And we girls had little guidance. There wasn't the tiniest smidgen of sex in *Girl* or *School Friend* – magazines from my youth, only a few strict prefects called Imogen or Monica and the occasional tomboy.

These publications have got us nowhere. I was talking to my friend Sylvia about Mrs Blood and her dead husband's sperm when Sylvia made a confession. 'I'm in my seventy-seventh year,' said she, 'and I still don't know where they get the sperm from.' Was there a permanent pool available, and where was it stored, or did it only appear on demand? What a disgrace that

I couldn't really explain it to her – *and* after all these years of criticising chaps for not having an inkling about the female body.

At least Sylvia and I are able to discuss these topics. Rosemary avoids them like the plague. At her school even *School Friend* was banned and taxi rides were considered quite disreputable. Rosemary was instructed never to enter a taxi with a boy. No one ever mentioned sperm or body parts, but there was talk of 'a vein of gold in a rock' that a girl might come across in later life. Rosemary was baffled. She could have done with a few copies of *More*, *Minx* and *Just Seventeen*.

Perhaps this is one area in which things have improved. My daughter is forever jumping boldly into taxis with boys. Off they go, waving their mobile phones and vile magazines and chattering blithely about sex, to rave and party. We are now frightfully up-to-date in our house. Even my mother is at it.

'They're talking about oral sex,' she cries, horrified but riveted to the telly, even before breakfast. Whatever did they teach them at *her* school?

Goodbye Senses

Sylvia's daughter entered the kitchen the other day and gave a cry of horror. Someone had made a vile smell. Of course it was the dog, but Sylvia hadn't smelt a thing. At seventy-six she is obviously losing another of her faculties.

'Something else to look forward to,' said the Daughter in a mocking way, and rushed out of the room holding her nose.

It would be easy to be downcast about this but I think Sylvia should be positive. The dog could be fainting in its own stench and Sylvia would be spared any unpleasantness. She could be imagining roses all the while. And look at these new scratch-and-sniff history books for children. Who wants to smell Henry VIII's gangrenous feet? Now Sylvia will be able to read these books to her great-nieces or possible future grandchildren in comfort. And as taste is 80 per cent smell, she will be able to eat up any old meal, however disgustingly cooked, and still smile appreciatively at the hostess.

Of course there are disadvantages. Her daughter has come rushing into the kitchen in a panic when the reek of escaped gas became overwhelming, but so far Sylvia has escaped unharmed. And she can't smell the lovely flowers in her garden. Last year she failed to smell the mahonia. Thinking there was something wrong with it, she added fertiliser rather lavishly and almost killed it. Just in time a friend smelt it and saved its life.

My mother, on the other hand, is often tormented by smell. 'I've got a very acute sense of smell,' she bellows, glaring at the source of the tiniest hint of body-odour, cigarette smoke or garlic. 'Who's been smoking/using the bathroom/frying fish?' she cries, rushing from her room with the air-freshener and spraying fiercely, clogging the house with a new stink and choking the dog.

All her life my mother has battled with smells: an uncle reeking of alcohol, visiting youths with smelly feet, colleagues with personal hygiene problems. Always she has spoken out boldly – advising, reprimanding and distributing Odorono roll-ons. Even now, sharp as ever and assailed by villainous stinks, my mother's nose gives her no respite. Our dustbins fester in the front garden, Gardener has sprinkled chicken-shit in the back, visiting cats foul the borders and the dog has a recurrent bowel disorder. Life is far more relaxing for Sylvia, even if she can't wander about her garden dreamily sniffing at the azaleas and wisteria any more. Meanwhile I am getting more and more short-sighted. I must almost poke my nose into the dinner to see the bones in my fish. Is this another faculty on the way out?

Old Friends, New Parties

I was wrong about my generation. They have not given up hope in the electoral process as I thought but are throwing themselves into politics. The coming election has whipped them into a frenzy. My friend Toad rang the other day and begged me to go to a meeting of the UK Independence Party. His wife Eleanor has become an enthusiastic convert and is dragging friends and relatives along to meetings. Toad himself is not convinced and naturally concerned about his wife's state of mind.

Once before a friend of ours joined a rabid and minute new party. Toad and I went along to inspect it and rescue her if necessary. This friend was weak and exhausted from campaigning and worrying desperately about the state of the world. Ours is perhaps a dangerous age, when one can look back over one's life and realise that it has been something of a waste of time. A radical new party seems just the thing to put things right.

Toad's wife did not need rescuing. She looked radiant and the meeting was packed out with people desperate to 'get out of the European Union, preserve the pound' and deal strictly with crime. Our gold is going to be lifted out of the Bank of England, piled onto lorries and driven off to Germany. Our pensions are going to be 'harmonised'. Terrifying news. Nothing could drag her away from this gripping stuff. She would stay to the very end, but the Toad and I sloped off exhausted for a tea-break. He was wearing a rather provocative French beret.

And Toad's wife is not the only one. I hear that another old friend of mine is standing as a candidate for the Natural Law Party, another is organising a European march against unemployment and another is campaigning like billy-o for the Labour Party in Kensington. Perhaps it is only me who has lost hope and thinks the world has had it. Perhaps it's time for a rethink and final struggle. I notice that all world leaders are about my age. So when the Labour Party rang to say would I stuff envelopes, canvass, drive people around on The Day and help in a neighbouring marginal seat, naturally I said yes.

Meanwhile, according to the Daughter's only politically active friend, it is Youth that is cynical. She tries to chat with her peers about the coming election but they either glaze over or leave the room. Only one responded.

'All politicians are two-faced bastards,' he roared from his squat.

A Turn for the Better

While I was out yesterday my mother had a horrid turn. Her eye began smarting and her left arm tingling, she called weakly for help but no one responded. Another drama was going on upstairs. Daughter had split her toe open, it poured blood, and while she screamed and searched wildly for plasters, her friends had carried on decorating the spare room, the pop music boomed on and no one could hear my mother. No wonder she panicked. The Grim Reaper could have snatched her away and no one would have been there to stop him.

Luckily I returned in the nick of time. The music was turned off, the toe stopped bleeding, the arm stopped tingling. A few hours of calm passed. Then the tingling started again. What a fright. I called the ambulance. Sometimes relaxation is not an option in our house. The tingling stopped. But the ambulance men were on their way. My mother tore off her rings again. 'Take my rings,' she commanded with her remaining strength. 'Hide them.'

Two charming, calm and saintly ambulance men arrived, held my mother's hand, gave her breathing instructions and were ever so kind. Naturally she burst into tears. They would take her to hospital for a check-up. My mother perked up tremendously. Not only would she be safe, but she would also get out of our hell-hole of a house for hours, maybe even days. She described our daily life in colourful detail to the ambulance men. They escorted her to the ambulance, all laughing and cracking jokes. I reminded my mother that she was meant to be ill, the National Health is run on a shoestring and the neighbours might be watching and wondering. Could she please try to look a little more poorly.

She couldn't care less. 'At least I'll be getting out of this ****house,' said she fiercely and staggered into the ambulance. Off she went to the Whittington. It was paradise. Everything was checked: chest X-rayed, blood pressure taken, heart monitored, pulses read, blood tested, consultants called. I followed later. My mother looked tremendously well. At one-forty-five a.m. she was at last allowed home. She felt tip-top and waved happily at the receptionist on her way out.

'Another satisfied customer,' she called. The receptionist looked rather gobsmacked. Clients are rarely so cheery and appreciative. My mother will be back soon for a twenty-four-hour check-up. She cannot wait. In the meantime she has had a thrilling evening, the Reaper has buzzed off, the weather is improving and the rings have gone on again. We live on a roller-coaster.

Flabby Fellows

Olga went out for a special lunch with a chum of hers last week to celebrate their joint birthdays. They chose a tremendously swizzy restaurant overlooking the Thames, rather gothic, with delightful ambience, charming waiters and very attractive-looking food which, sadly, tasted rather dull.

Then they looked around at the other diners and noticed that they were nearly all middle-aged businessmen. Their flesh was soft and pink with no apparent muscle tone. 'You know the sort,' says Olga. 'If you pressed it in, it wouldn't come out again.' There was one woman at a nearby table, also very smooth and pink, as if she'd been gone over with an electric buffer, but she did look a tiny bit more healthy than the chaps, as if she at least walked to her car.

It wouldn't have been such a tragedy if the lunches had been divine. Then these men's lives would have been short but glorious, filled with exquisite tastes and experiences, but if this place was anything to go by, then they had all ruined their health for nothing. Olga had a dismal thought: that all over the country at midday, thousands of podgy men are waddling from one mediocre restaurant to the next and heading straight for a premature death.

She felt that once upon a time these men must have been teenagers like her own son, skinny and energetic, running after footballs and girls. Now here they were turned into capons with soft baby faces. What could have happened to them? It threw Olga and her friend into a gloom. Being rather thin, they will probably shrink and go the way of Mother Theresa, swathed in wrinkles, their skin gathered in frills. So will I.

There is no escape from it. One way or another the body is going to wear out and change shape. But what a pity the mind and body deteriorate at different rates. I spotted myself on video the other day. Such a fright! My top lip seemed to have disappeared and I closely resembled one of my aunties in her eighties. I don't feel that old. No wonder that people are forever moaning on about this. There is the personality, still feeling twenty years old or so, but the body is galloping on downhill, mouldering, thickening or shrivelling.

And there is always a mirror about to keep us in the picture. Naturally my mother is not keen on mirrors. 'Bloody hell,' she moans, looking at her wizened reflection. In her mind she is still the sprightly dashing young creature in jodhpurs who whizzed about on a motorbike or in a Clyno car, slim, glamorous and wrinkle-free. Now here she is, trapped in a lumbering and crumpled body. It does not reflect her personality.

There is nothing like a surprise reflection to ruin one's day. I notice that shop windows often act as a mirror, especially those at an angle. There I am, walking along in a carefree way, feeling young in spirit and perhaps planning to buy a garment, when WHAM! A sloping window flashes the truth before me, and in profile, my least favourite view of the self, and my walk and shopping are ruined. I could carry on and try a shop, but the fitting room mirrors would only say the same thing again.

Olga's report has depressed us all, but at least she has learned from her mistake. For their next birthday outing she and her chum will cycle off to a frugal vegetarian restaurant in Dalston recommended by a very thin gardener.

The Final Frontier

I hear that one may now be popped into a funeral canister and shot out into space. And it only costs $5,000. This is a snip and no dearer than your average reasonably posh funeral. My mother is not interested. She would much prefer to be scattered over a rose bush in Hove, next to my father.

Good job. Imagine if everyone went zooming out into space after death. The astronauts might be working away on the Hubble telescope and suddenly a funeral canister might zip by and knock them off their floating work bench.

'Look out Pete, here comes another one. It's like a *!*!ing rubbish tip out here!'

Down here on earth I've spotted a far more moving funeral. On top of the hearse was a giant yellow and white tea-pot made of flowers, with the large letters GRAN alongside and also in flowers. I wept all the way home. But my mother would never allow such a thing. She has banned flowers. 'Bloody waste of money,' she has shouted over and over again. 'They can send donations to . . .'

Perhaps she is right. I hear that funerals are now hugely expensive and all secretly run by Service Corporation International. Those little funeral parlours in the High Street that you think are independent are a deception, puppet undertakers taking orders from someone greedy thousands of miles away.

This is enough to make anyone sensible hide their wallet under the mattress and order a cardboard coffin. That's what

Fielding's mother is going to do, and very sensible too. I hear that someone else has sprinkled their communist father over Marx's grave, and a friend of Rosemary's had just decided to be a sapling, only to hear that planning permission had been given for a bypass over her chosen spot.

Advance planning and paying seems to be the mode. Rosemary has paid in advance to go on top of her husband, to make up for all the times she wouldn't do it during his lifetime. This is far more constructive than having your head removed from your body and frozen. That is not much of an answer. A new body would one day be grown on to the head and you'd have to go through the whole ghastly performance again, probably wearing different trousers.

I shall scatter the dog over the Heath, and as for me, I would like to be sprinkled on a lilac and appear smelling divine for a couple of weeks a year. Forget the black horses, and no canisters thank you, just in case anyone wants to know.

Period Dramas

My friend Olivia is fed-up with what may be a rather grim feature of the menopause. She is in the middle of her second three-week-long torrential period. She is a temporary incontinent encased in nappies and her bedroom and bathroom seem to belong to World War Two. Her bath is constantly full of soaking clothes and linen and she is terrified to sit on anyone else's chairs, sofas or car seats in case the floodgates open and ruin their upholstery.

Worse still, Olivia must keep this ghastly ordeal a secret. Even nowadays, when sex, violence and condoms are all the rage and people are able to chatter in a forthright way about all manner of sexual deviances and proclivities, the dread period is still shrouded in mystery.

On the telly it is fresh, blue, attractive and under control. Women in the throes of it bounce around in white shorts looking fit, young, cheery and smart. But Olivia is trudging around in a bate leaking and spending the bulk of her day in the lavatory, or planning how to get to the next one. And she isn't the only one. Many give up and lie about writhing and clutching hot-water bottles. Then there's the pain, the expense, the disgrace if anyone spots it, then the ruined clothes, general public revulsion or official banishment to cleansing baths. Even Rosemary is revolted by it.

'That's quite enough of that, thank-you,' she snaps, should I mention it, and runs to the end of the garden.

In my youth I thought it might even things up a bit if men were to have periods every fortnight for the rest of their lives, starting *immediately*. Then a few years ago I discovered, while reading a bedtime story to my daughter, that it doesn't have to be like this. In America, said the story, girls sometimes rejoice at the onset of the menses and even hold celebratory parties. But the Daughter begged not to have a party. We do, after all, live in England, where girls will probably be keeping it a secret till doomsday.

How does one break free? Even this article is a lie. It wasn't Olivia really, it was me, plodding around swathed in nappies and trying not to mention blood. Apparently women often do. Olga had the same problem and acupuncture cured it. I have followed her example. It worked once, will it work again? Is it fibroids? Is it cancer? Is it hysterectomy time? Or is it just normal? Answers please, plus names and photographs.

Bring Back Call-Up

One can get sick of Youth. We are forever pandering to them and making excuses for them: poor things, they have no future, no job security, dollops of stress, pressure and anxiety. No wonder they diddle about, get drunk, stoned, crack up, drop out, are ill-mannered, aggressive and always want new trainers.

I feel the same old words welling up in my throat: 'In my day people said please and thank-you, wore plimsols and Clark's shoes, ate up their greens, learnt Latin and never swore at grown-ups.'

Meanwhile, no allowances are made for people of my age. This is the age when one behaves properly. All the rest have excuses: children because they're children, Youth because they're under stress, old age because they're old, but here in the middle we must carry on being reasonable, the carthorses of society, while everyone else runs amok.

Perhaps I am in a sour mood because this is a particularly trying time of year when Youth are doing their exams. The Daughter is struggling with A levels. Last night she let out a scream. At once the phone rang. A sympathetic neighbouring youth was calling. He had recognised the sound – the pain of the Last Night Before Course Work is Given In.

All over England doors are slamming, Youth are tantrum-ming, teachers are tearing their hair out and I am having my Martinis earlier and earlier in the day. As I may not scream in the home because I want to keep things lovely and calm, I have a scream in the car. In the roar of traffic, if I keep the windows shut, no one can hear. They may see a strange-looking woman with her mouth open and face distorted, but think no more of it.

Today I met my friend Janet on the Heath. She too has come out for a scream and is a slave to her children. Her A level daughter goes white and silent with fright, her son spends whole holidays in his pyjamas glaring at television.

Next door Rosemary's A-level son, the Perfect Boy, is not living up to his name. He too is glued to the telly, even through *Blue Peter*, and has eagerly followed their banana cake recipe. What exams? What revision? 'Bring back call-up,' shouts Rosemary in despair.

Meanwhile my mother hides in her room, especially on exam days, handing out the odd chocolate. But this is a breakthrough year for parents. It is the first time that we, the elderly, are looking forward to the end of term and Glastonbury.

New Technology

Olga had a fearful technology experience last week. She tried to ring Olivia but an annoying answerphone robot-woman asked her to leave a message. Olga was enraged.

'Get rid of that *!*!*ing stupid BT answerphone,' she screamed and slammed the phone down. Straightaway her phone rang. It was the robot-woman, who asked Olga if she was sure she wished to leave that message, then played it back to her.

Olga found this rather unnerving. Was the robot-woman listening out for obscenities or for criticism of BT? If Olga had repeated that rude word, would the robot-woman have rung her back again? They could have been on the phone all day. All over Britain people could be swearing at BT answerphones and arguing with pretend voices for hours on end if they so chose.

The new technology is a nightmare process. No wonder it upsets my mother. In her day the muffin-man came round with a tray on his head and the milkman had a horse and cart. She must now battle with call-barring and unbarring, Call Waiting, word-processing, microwaving, videoing and now the new cordless telephone, with its lights going on and off and odd blipping noises. And our house is fizzing with televisions. They twinkle and blare from almost every room.

Only the Daughter eagerly embraces modern technology. She has saved up and brought herself a mobile phone. It is free at weekends. She may now talk continually for forty-eight hours, risking a brain tumour as the radio waves pulse into her skull, while the technophobe mother and grandmother flap around in a panic.

Yesterday Rosemary flew into a temper over my Call Waiting and slammed the phone down. She often does this. I now know that if the waiting caller has failed to wait, it is probably Rosemary.

I dial 1471 to check. Yes it was. I ring back. All this complexity and Rosemary only wanted to borrow an onion. Why did she not come and knock at the door like they used to do in the old days? And she is incensed with BT for putting me on her friends and family list.

'How dare they tell me who my friends are?' she snaps. But never mind. When we have all been driven terminally mad by the telephone, Toshiba will have a robot-nurse ready to care for us. It will plod through the wards, from bed to bed, displaying menus on its monitor, bringing dinners on trays and presumably whacking the disobedient with a mechanical arm. 'Eat – up – your – greens – or – else.' Confused elderly persons will be tracked by satellite.

I dare not tell Olga about it.

Election Party

Rosemary comes trudging home from work exhausted. Apparently all her colleagues and friends are exhausted too, particularly those of our age. She blames the election, although it was weeks ago. It was all too much for us, says she – the weeks of tension, the preceding eighteen years of gloom and final thrilling result. We are all emotionally drained, and not used to staying up all night partying, screaming and drinking heavily, especially on a Thursday.

We did have our election party in the end. What fun. All those little red bands winging across the screen, all those deposed ministers, the Celts' rebellion, the Mellor/Goldsmith squabble. Naturally we all screamed a lot, us downstairs, my mother up in her room with visitors, Daughter and friends on the top floor.

Suddenly, at one-fifteen a.m., the door bell rang tremendously loudly. It was two rather crotchety policemen ordering us to stop making a noise. Unknown to me, those teenagers upstairs, first-time voters fuelled by alcohol, had been screaming far more loudly than I imagined, with the front window open. There they all were in a drunken, roaring heap on the bed, celebrating.

Rosemary is not entirely right about the election. It has rather perked some of us up, whereas the young seem to be grinding us down. This summer is a worsening nightmare. As their exams draw nearer, Daughter and her chums are being driven half-mad by the unaccustomed forced labour, escaping from parents up and down the street and running to their friends' houses for a scream and a cigarette. Election Day was the perfect opportunity for prolonged screaming.

Today the Daughter ran out in a wild mood, slamming the front door ferociously. The house shuddered. My mother shrieked from her bunker on the first floor, 'Who's slamming the front door?' She knows, of course, but also needs to have a scream. The stress is telling on all of us. My mother is in a particularly anxious mood, further terrified by the recent news of a woman who gave birth at sixty-three. She is now concerned about my welfare.

'Be careful,' she cries whenever a chap hoves into view. 'It can still happen.'

What a frightful prospect. When the poor sixty-three-year-old woman is eighty-one, she will be going through A levels with her child. Has she thought this through carefully? Has she seen large girls and boys revising, screeching and rushing from house to house? Or grizzling with panic? And if she has to miss a night's sleep for elections, she'll be done for.

I Should Have Danced All Night

It's difficult to leave an elderly mother alone at night. Will she still be with us when I return? Will the angina have struck in my absence? Stuck in the house like this I long to rush out into the night and go dancing. But where can I go for a dance at my age? Most venues are black holes crammed with youth, where squillion-decibel music shatters the ear-drums and thuds through the body. When one is fifty-four, this is a debilitating experience. There is also a risk that among the crowds my own child may be lurking and sneering with her chums.

Last year we tried Seventies Night at the Camden Palace. We arrived at nine o'clock but the place was empty. We danced alone. By eleven-thirty, just as the first guests were drifting in, we had to go home because it was past our bedtime.

Then we tried again – to a big band in Brixton. At least it wasn't packed only with the young. Whole families, even grandmas and babies were there, all jumping about, but the decibels were still a problem. To dull the pain and reduce damage I stuffed tissue into my ears, but it went too far and I couldn't retrieve it. Gardener had to take me home and remove it by torchlight with pointy medical tweezers, which rather spoilt our evening.

But one tends to forget pain and trauma and try things all over again, rather like childbirth, so when Olga and her chums asked me to go dancing just down the road, I said yes. Olga booked tickets.

The day arrived. It just so happened that I was ever so tired, my hair looked unusually frightful and I no longer wished to go dancing. I plodded on with my evening. Perhaps I would return to life at the venue. Everything was in my favour: sound level tolerable, music divine and the groovy middle-aged and elderly were there in droves, some grey, some bald, thin trembly ones, fat bouncy ones, even some with sticks, all throwing themselves about.

Olga and her chums danced wildly. Even Fielding began to shuffle around. But I couldn't. I stood weedily in a corner with my half pint of shandy, rigid and crippled by inhibition.

What a disappointment. For years I had waited for such an opportunity: conditions were just right, the joint rocking, everyone jumping about, clapping and yelling, and there I was unable to move a single muscle. And my legs ached. I leant on a railing looking glum and prim and dreamed of the perfect evening – at home watching the telly with my cocoa and ninety-year-old mother.

Bad Language

Rosemary is having trouble with her students. As the terms pass they grow increasingly mutinous, and who can blame them? Rosemary is forever on about grammar and vocabulary, and is further cursed with a posh voice. She can't help it. She went to a strict girls' school, then a girls only university where students drank cocoa in the evening and drifted round the library in dressing-gowns and slippers. She has retained some of her antiquated vocabulary.

Only recently she used the words *obdurate* and *hiatus*. The students grew sullen. 'Speak proper English, Rosemary,' they snarled, rather disappointing her. She had hoped that their eyes might light up at the sound of unfamiliar words, that they would grasp their biros and eagerly note down this useful new vocabulary and with it enrich their future essays, but no such luck.

I must say I agree with Rosemary on this one. How is anyone to improve if they will not learn? We often moan about this on our dog-walks, two elderly reactionaries talking about apostrophes, agreement, subordinate clauses, sloppy spelling and impoverished vocabularies. Rosemary has banned her students from using certain key words and phrases: *issues about, the reason is because*, and such like. It gets her nowhere, except up before a complaints board.

But Rosemary battles on. She has adapted to modern methods and invites criticism, or 'feedback', as one must nowadays.

'Go on,' she says. 'You may criticise. Say I'm old-fashioned.' And then to stir things up a big she badgers them with Latin roots, pretending that it will help them to remember meaning. They all beg to have a different tutor.

Obviously this problem is preying on her mind. She recently spotted a mistake in the baker's window: 'Scottish £5 notes not exepted', and felt impelled to go in and put them right. Rosemary did apologise in a grovelling way, explaining that she was a teacher and had got into the habit of correcting spellings, but the bakers were very surly about it and Rosemary came home feeling wretched.

But she won't give up. Last week she took advantage of the election result to introduce the words *hubris* and *nemesis*. Naturally the students were scathing.

'There must be an easier way of talking about getting those shits out,' they said crossly. Rosemary is getting nowhere, even though our new government and future king are nagging for improvement. Here she is trying to combat 'banality, cliché and casual obscenity' and this is her reward. She left the class-room in something of a temper, calling over her shoulder, 'Education, education, education.'

Where's the Gravy?

My mother returns from her club in a joyous mood. This woman she's never spoken to before suddenly started chatting and bemoaning her daughter's and granddaughter's behaviour. Both address her disrespectfully and use vile language.

'Your daughter?' asked my mother, horrified. 'Granddaughter yes, but daughter, NO! My daughter would *never* speak to me like that!'

This was a treat for my mother. Usually it is other women gaping at her saying, 'My granddaughter would *never* behave like that!', or staring as if shell-shocked at my clothing or coiffure. But I have now become a paragon in her eyes. It is sometimes uplifting to hear that others are worse off than yourself.

My friend Jacqueline's mother suddenly fell down while pottering round the garden and broke her arm. She has now come to stay with Jacqueline and be looked after. But what bad luck, just as she moved in the builders moved out, halfway through the job, as builders are wont to do, and left them without a kitchen.

Jacqueline now has no oven and her family and temporarily disabled mother live on a building site. Still, she is doing her best, and this weekend barbecued the dinner, peeled her mother's new potatoes as requested, cut up the meat lovely and small and carried it up on a tray.

'Where's the gravy,' asked her mother crossly. She will only accept conventional dinners and anything wildly out of the ordinary, like rice, is rejected out of hand.

My mother is thrilled by all this. Compared to Jacqueline's mother she is tremendously easy-going and will eat all manner of adventurous dinners without complaint. She now shouts 'Where's the gravy?' in a mocking way at the beginning of every meal and will brook no criticism of her own family.

Yesterday Rosemary unwisely criticised my celery and walnut soup. She had contributed a celery and come to collect her portion, just as my mother was having hers. 'Tastes of nothing,' said my mother disdainfully. 'Where's the soya sauce?'

Rosemary tasted it. A stark choice loomed. She must agree with me or my mother. Unwisely she chose to suck up to my mother and agreed with her criticism. Wrong. My mother managed to contain herself until Rosemary had gone home, then she let rip.

'She can make her own bloody soup if she doesn't like it!' she yelled, drinking up the ghastly stuff. 'Where's the salt,' she moaned, screwing up her nose. 'Don't make this again. It's very bland.' She glared defiantly. 'No one can criticise my daughter,' she snapped, 'except me.'

Minimalist Shopping

Something else to look forward to when one is old and alone: minimalist shopping. My neighbour across the road has started it already. Now his children have grown up he no longer needs a giant barrowload of provisions from the supermarket, just the odd snack for himself.

This must be a tremendous saving. Only last week I spent £179.63 in Sainsbury's. I stuffed it all into the car, came home, unloaded it, Daughter rammed it into the fridge, freezer and larder and now, just a few days later, it is gone. Mainly down the throats of the young. My mother and I have seen only a few crumbs of it.

But worse still, whatever isn't snatched and eaten instantly has to be cooked or prepared in some way: chopped, mixed, whisked, peeled, taken in and out of cupboards, spilt, cleared up, eaten or scraped off plates, then off for another truckload. I am on a treadmill.

So one day, when I live all alone, I shall just trundle up the road with my spinster basket on wheels to buy minimum requirements, and live on salads and the odd potato. And as I shall be retired I'll be able to shop a little at a time whenever I please and not in one gargantuan three-hour outing into hell after work.

Olga now has the chance to do this. Her son has left to live with his beloved and she is alone at home. Oddly enough, she still hangs round supermarkets, suffering from what seem to be withdrawal symptoms. Off she goes with the large trolley, wandering up and down the aisles, pretending that she's still an efficient wife and mother, looking at all the things she used to buy, but when she reaches the checkout, only a few small items are rattling around her trolley, and last week she spent just £23.

This could sound heart-rending but Olga rather likes it. She particularly liked the £23 at the end. However, there are dangers when shopping alone. I once knew an unpleasant fellow who would lurk at strategic shelves watching out for lone female shoppers. He would then pretend to be charming, meet them again in aisle after aisle and then invite them out, rather like the Wolf and Red Riding Hood. When one is in a dream at the cheese counter and doing something normal like shopping, one does not expect to meet a monster. On the other hand my friend X, aged fifty, met the love of her life in Sainsbury's. Soon her trolley was full up again.

Bottoms

Olivia was about to try on a tremendously chic frock the other day when she happened to catch sight of her back view in the fitting room mirror. What a fright! She had four buttocks! Fat pulped over her knicker elastic dividing each side of her bottom into two. What used to be visible-panty-line was now glaring-panty-gorge, rather like a motorway cutting through a mountain range of blubber. Olivia sat down on her ghastly bottom and wept.

I was rather surprised by this news. I have always thought Olivia strikingly elegant in her tasteful, flowing garments, but now she tells me that they conceal a jellybaby body, the dual bottom *and* a gigantic bosom which, if left to its own devices, flobs down to her waist, along with her chins.

Perhaps Olivia has a touch of body dysmorphic disorder. Her single chin is in fact in the normal place and I have never noticed the giant bosom.

'I wear minimiser bras,' whispered Olivia, looking desolate. She is not alone. Although relatively thin, I too feel tragic in fitting rooms. I recently tried on a rather dashing leopard skin swimming costume. It divided my bottom up, just as Olivia's knickers had done, but into flaps and folds rather than bulges.

It has come as a dreadful shock to both of us to find our flesh hanging rather than rippling. It all seems rather sudden. One minute we can wear shorts, the next minute it's jellabas only. For a few days we blamed ourselves. Perhaps we should have exercised, rather than sneering at joggers and all forms of sport. But Olga has done her exercises: cycling everywhere, practising yoga, dashing off on rigorous mountain-climbing holidays, and her body has still gone the way of all flesh.

This week she bought a sequinned top in an Oxfam shop. She thought she could pretend to be someone old-fashioned and look ironic and amusing, as well as smart. So she took it home, flung it on, approached the mirror and there was an elderly creature with a scraggy turkey neck in a suitably strange old garment with no irony at all.

Meanwhile it is summer and the Young are out and about in teensy vests and skirts and shorts looking heavenly, with no wrinkles and only one chin and bottom apiece. Luckily Olivia and I have had a party to go to. We wrapped ourselves up in our smart new clothes and had a lovely time, despite our awful bottoms. But next time we shop we shall go together. When you need support, always take a friend.

Galley Slaves

My mother is still the resident chef. Thank goodness. I am increasingly sick to death of cooking and the kitchen. Today she staggered downstairs to make chicken soup, one of her specialities.

'What will you do when I'm dead?' she cried, leaning exhausted on the draining board. 'What will you eat?'

'Vegetarian snacks, uncooked.'

'What about HER,' groans my mother, referring to her voracious granddaughter. 'She'll want dinners.'

But by the time my mother is departed, the granddaughter will have left school and have time to slave over her own meals. I shall insist that she does so. This is my new resolution.

My mother has no confidence in it. She feels that my authority over the Daughter is negligible, so she battles on with the cooking, knowing that should she stop we shall all revert to eating rubbish snacks, become anaemic and succumb to disease. This is her fate – to drag herself about until the very end, ensuring that her two infants are adequately fed.

To the outsider I may seem heartless and wicked, forcing my ninety-year-old mother to be galley slave, but surprisingly, she is still keen on cooking. I cannot understand why. Even Rosemary has begun to find cooking tiresome. For years she has cooked vigorously, and even, when her husband was alive, regularly produced three contrasting meals at once: curry for the husband, non-curry for the son and vegetarian delicacies for the daughters. She herself would pick at bits of everyone else's dinner. But now she can scarcely be bothered.

On Sunday I took my mother to visit my old friend Jacqueline for lunch. She too has spent thirty-five years sweating in the kitchen, catering for her husband and three children. What bad luck that my mother has brought fishcake ingredients with her. After lunch she springs up and begins cooking away all over again with Jacqueline as assistant. Soon they both stagger from the kitchen, eyes watering from the grated onions and both stinking of fried fish. It rather got up my mother's nose that I was relaxing in front of *East Enders'* Omnibus, but I have had the fishcake lesson and experience countless times and it is my day off.

This has been a disappointing area of my mother's life, to have had a sullen daughter who scuttles away when recipes are mentioned. But what if I had loved cooking and we had been in competition? One thing I do appreciate about a kitchen – you can only have one head chef.

Sausage Rolls

My mother is off to a nursing home with a chum of hers. What bliss to get away from our home and its residents: my mess, the Daughter's A level stress, the dribbling dog and various annoying visitors. Instead she will have two weeks' tidiness, peace and her own peer group. It is called respite care.

Nowadays one has to be frightfully careful, what with all these hair-raising tales of the elderly being slapped about or scalded while their relatives aren't looking, but her friend Esther, after months of searching, has finally found somewhere suitable.

This is my mother's first proper break from the Household from Hell in over two years. She is thrilled. Off we go, out of town and into the fresh air. The chosen residence is surrounded by green lawns, the furnishings are tasteful, the rooms immaculate and staff charming. But wait! There is no bidet. My mother is bitterly disappointed. And a shower instead of a bath, and a slippery floor! Staff point out the special shower seat to soothe my mother, just in time for supper.

I accompany her to the dining room. The atmosphere is not vibrant. No one is chatting. Many are too poorly to chat. All residents are pallid. My mother is the only person with her lipstick on. Worse still, sausage rolls are on the menu. I suspect that sausage rolls might play havoc with an ancient digestive system, but they do tend to pop up on the menus of such establishments, together with white bread, moistureless chicken and wodgy puddings.

I leave my mother sitting bravely at the dining table and drive home in despair. Compare this British regime with the Pacific Home, California, where Rosemary's mother is spending half the year. Not a sausage roll in sight. Menu includes peach nectar, cinnamon toast, green beans on apple-walnut turkey, seafood basket, avocado salad and chicken wings and wine every Friday night. And an Ocean Front dining room, heated pool, sandy beach, billiards, library, Hobby Shop and other play areas. How depressing to find that the Pacific Home costs half the price of my mother's establishment. I am not pleased

Next day I ring for a progress report.

'I told them where to stuff their sausage rolls,' said my mother. Luckily bridge games have been organised and her chum has arrived. But will she last the fortnight? And will she ever speak to Rosemary's mother again?

Oils of War

I ring my mother for a report on conditions in the nursing home in which I have so heartlessly left her. Grim news. The food continues fairly execrable and staff tell my mother that they are underpaid, overworked, and as from this week, may have no more free meals. Naturally they are mutinous and leaving in droves. No one has time to take my mother and her chum Esther downstairs and out into the sunny garden. For one week they have been marooned on the first floor.

As we chat on the telephone I hear wild and prolonged screaming in the background.

'Someone's screaming for help,' says my mother calmly. The screaming continues. No staff appear. We chatter on. Yesterday my mother ordered tomatoes vinaigrette, but the tomatoes appeared alone. More screaming. My mother is stuck in Colditz without a salad dressing. For this, we and the local council are paying £500 a week between us.

'Heee-eeellp,' goes the screaming. In desperation my mother prepares to investigate herself. Just in time a nurse appears. For £500 one can have one week full board in the charming Greek island hotel with turquoise swimming pool where Daughter and I once spent a delightful holiday eating peaches and grapes for breakfast, and salads awash with dressing, day and night.

I may seem to be going overboard about salad dressings, but without a daily measure of olive oil my mother's life is scarcely worth living. Also we are part of Europe now and the days of yellow Salad Cream are meant to be over.

But my mother is determined to stick it out. She cannot desert her chum, who cannot go home because her daughter, who cares for her, is abroad on holiday. At least they have had two bridge games and some passable smoked mackerel. And they can chat non-stop.

Luckily Esther's other daughter has brought vital supplies of oil and taken them both out for tea. A sniff of open air at last. I hear that in H. M. Prisons one hour daily in the open air is statutory. My mother might have been better off in Risley (cost: £480 per week, baths, bingo and all meals included). Perhaps she would like to escape early? Shall I collect her *before* the last lunch on Sunday?

'No!' my mother shouts defiantly. 'It's roast beef. I'm having it. I've bloody paid for it.' She has always been a determined woman.

Gardening to the End

As I grow older and older I become more and more keen on the garden. It is a scented paradise enhanced by birdsong and the croaking of froggies from the pond. A charming exodus of witsy baby frogs jumps diagonally across the lawn and bees hum about the flowers. To reach this heaven I need only shuffle a few steps from my kitchen door.

No wonder the elderly are prone to gardening. Last year's Chelsea show was choc-full of them, Rosemary and Olga and Sylvia are endlessly fiddling in their gardens and so is my mother.

But a garden can be a dangerous emotional minefield. My mother and I are forever battling over choice of plants and methods. I move her favourite poppies, she hacks at my favourite rose bush. There it is hanging gracefully over the pond, I go shopping briefly, I return to find it looking like a mad person's haircut. Rosemary gangs up with my mother. 'Nothing wrong with it,' she snaps. 'I don't know what you're on about.' She perhaps envies my Alstroemeria. It is more attractively coloured than hers.

And now the runner-beans are climbing over the wall. My mother now fears that the neighbour, whom we don't like, may get some of our beans. This cannot happen. The beans must be redirected. And the other neighbour, whom we do like, has allowed his Convolvulus to rampage all over our roses. Soon my mother's patience will snap and she will never lend him the bottle-opener again.

Things are even worse for Rosemary. She has been forced to build a large trellis on one side to block off the neighbour who will keep on chatting and relentlessly singing along to hymns. But Rosemary's waterlily has flowered and mine hasn't, although we bought them at the same time in the same place. I am furious.

Our gardens are fraught with tension and under constant threat. Squirrels have chewed the tops off Rosemary's pinks, eaten my strawberries and torn up my thyme, cats have pooed on my newly planted Rudbeckia, the dog has weed on the lawn and the snails are champing through everything.

In fact the garden is a battleground. Over it one can fight one's friends, relatives, neighbours, the Gardener and the elements. It develops diseases, attracts pests, causes rows, needs constant attention and is all-consuming. We need never go anywhere else.

Could Do Better

Daughter has finished her A levels. What a relief for all of us. This is a time that we have all longed for – a stress-free period when the Daughter and her peers, no longer burdened by homework and anxiety, will be free to help with the washing-up, tidying, laundry, cooking and shopping. Tension and screaming in our home will stop and a generally sunny atmosphere will prevail.

For years I have clung to this dream like a drowning woman and at last it has come true. Daughter has been washing-up, tidying and shopping *and* she has a job. But my mother is still not thrilled. She tends to clash with the Daughter over how much domestic work should be done by someone of eighteen. Their opinions differ wildly.

After years of slaving alone I am weedily grateful for any scrap of assistance in the home, but my mother is more demanding. Over the years she has noted the number of chores not done and it has rankled like a festering sore, reinfected after every meal and pile of laundry, until now, when the poison has surfaced like a giant boil, nearly bursting and not to be soothed by little patches of washing-up here and there.

The boil is further inflamed by my mother's own memories of childhood: her father, a charming wastrel, gambling and disappearing, her mother slaving in a market, herself slogging away looking after the little brother and sister, her horrid home-made knitted red petticoats, the mockery at school. Now here is her grandchild swanning about town, her wardrobe immense, hair highlighted, mobile phone peeping and exotic holidays planned. To balance the books a huge amount of housework, drudgery and charming behaviour is required.

Foolishly I point out the improvement to my mother. 'Look,' I squeal, thrilled by the novelty. 'She's done the washing-up! She's hung up her clothes! Her room's tidy! She's got up and gone to work!'

'About time too,' roars my mother. 'I should bloody well think so.' She cannot get the hang of positive reinforcement. It is a new-fangled idea, miles across the generation crater and she cannot leap that far.

'Next time,' I instruct, 'Say "*How lovely. Thank you!*" Do not use a sarcastic tone.' My mother sneers rebelliously. Our home is still a war zone, the kitchen is the front line, with no chance of a stress-free life – just the occasional cease-fire. But I hope one day for a united household. Just another little dream of mine.

Gap Year

I hear from my old friend Malcolm that his son, now eighteen, is going the way of all sons – off to Tunisia with a lump of hash and then on to a life sentence in a foreign jail. It is the beginning of his Gap Year. I have learned to dread these two words. The Daughter is forever dragging them up and planning a terrifying world tour.

Only last week she missed a connection to the Hebrides and was marooned in Glasgow overnight. Naturally she phoned from the station sobbing with panic. Several nearby families that I barely knew than had to be summoned by a complex network of telephone calls to rescue the Daughter. And she had cleverly managed to fritter £40 before even reaching her destination. How ever will she manage in the teeming capital cities and train terminals or remote jungles and mountains of Abroad?

Rosemary and I feel that the wrong generation is having a Gap Year. We should be having it instead, and round about now is the time, after children, A levels, caring for elderly parents and decades of work and worry. We desperately need a relaxing Gap before the grandchildren arrive and our children come knocking at the door begging for babysitters. Once the grown-up children are functioning independently and the elderly parents are no more, we must take a break, before this next avalanche of demands and while we still have a smidgen of energy left.

169

Meanwhile, Gap Year horror stories pour in, reinforcing our plan: X's son was mugged in Naples, nose punched in, passport and credit-cards stolen. He was forced to ring home for comfort and assistance; Y's son tripped in a remote jungle area, banged his head on a rock and was dragged unconscious through dense foliage to hospital; Rosemary's daughter was cruelly overworked as a nanny in Spain, her passport confiscated and wages withheld by the wicked employers. Rosemary received scores of reverse-charge phone calls, embassies had to be called and the daughter released. Once freed, the daughter's foot was run over by a refuse lorry as she snoozed in her sleeping bag on a foreign sea-shore.

Frankly, Rosemary and I have had enough of all this. Where did this silly idea come from? I suspect the grasping airlines with their tempting eight-stop £900 world tour for the Under-Twenty-ones. How about a similar bargain for the Over-Fifty-ones? Fat chance.

Party Politics

Last week my mother was ninety-one. She woke up suicidal. How can one be merry with a hernia, a gammy leg and piles? She dragged herself to the bathroom. There in the mirror was a wrinkled face surrounded by wisps of grey hair. My mother moaned in a heart-rending way and staggered back to bed.

People kept ringing up and coming round in hordes, singing Happy Birthday in an annoying way and showering her with presents, but it did no good. In between visitors she stubbed her toe, discovered that she has grown too fat for her best dresses, felt sick and tired and would rather have been twenty-one. Or dead.

Her new blouse was a disappointment, her chocolate cake too dry and her new shoes too tight. Still the visitors trudged in and out with cards, flowers and presents, but they were mainly my friends, because most of my mother's friends are no more. So she battled with terminal depression until lunch-time. Then off we went to a charming café and ate salads in the sun and gradually my mother perked up. Only ten hours to go and the hated birthday would be over.

In fact in our house only the Daughter is wild about birthdays. She is eighteen and mad on partying. This year she hired a venue, invited hundreds and they all danced, drank heavily and screamed in a pit of hell until the early hours. I visited briefly and left with impaired hearing. What thrilled her particularly about this birthday was that she might officially drink herself under the table. To her a birthday means presents, luxury and being able to officially do what your mother has always told you not to do: leave school, earn money, fritter it, have sex, tattoo your whole body and marry a wastrel.

Now my birthday is looming, my waistline has left me forever, the dog's time on earth is running out, but Rosemary is still nagging for some sort of celebration. She has recently embarked on a thrilling round of sixtieth-birthday parties at which the food is exquisite because everyone is showing off how well they have done in life. Then together they all wander down memory lane while they still have some memory to speak of.

Secretly I am rather keen on birthdays. They show that I have somehow lasted fifty-four years. Only thirty-seven years to go and I too shall have mobility and digestive problems. Rosemary is right. I should perhaps party while I still can.

Big Train Set

Rosemary and I are increasingly depressed about the way the world is going. Fairly pointless projects costing unknown billions of pounds are popping up everywhere, while gallons of the world's money cascades down the pan. First Mir, then the British Library, numerous space probes, and fiddling about on Mars and now the ghastly Dome, built to temporarily house God knows what. And we are in a frenzy over the Millennium. Why? It's a relatively small millennium confined to Christians. It isn't the Chinese, Jewish or Atheist Millennium.

Luckily the Dome costs a snip compared to the squillions being frittered on Mir, while down below the bulk of the Russian populace are half-starved, drunk and maddened by it all, their army unpaid, their trains sluggish, their orphans clogging the streets and their lakes poisoned. Good job my Grandma left early and came to England, otherwise I too would be living on porridge and potatoes while my Leaders gazed up at the stars.

At our age Rosemary and I can spot the decline, but John Glenn, now seventy-five, has learnt nothing. He is off into space again. Why? At his age he ought to know better. It will speed up his osteoporosis, if he has it, and anyway space is fairly dull. Mars is all dreary rocks, there is nothing much around except the odd flying bullet of rubbish or dagger of frozen urine. John could easily be shot or stabbed while floating about up there and his outing would be just another waste of time and money.

Meanwhile, down here on the ground, a race of giant rats has developed, fed on fast-food scraps and carrying new and deadly diseases through Camden Town, where an atmosphere of mess, wretchedness, dirt and despair prevails. Could not a little money be spent on general cleansing before the selection of sparkling new millennium monstrosities arrives? I notice that the same old gang is building them, Foster, Rogers et al., and although I try very hard not to, I can't help noticing that they are all chaps. There are chaps on Mir and chaps (plus one woman) in the Mars exploration office, cheering and congratulating each other like mad, naming rocks and playing with the ultimate remote-controlled toy car.

But in case any of these fellows have a few spare minutes or millions, we have an old train set down here that needs mending. It is called the London Underground. Has anyone noticed? Hallo out there!

Noise Nuisance

As I grow older I long for extensive periods of absolute silence. There is no such thing where I live. One can only experience calm wearing ear-plugs and heavily sedated.

Last Saturday I was woken at three a.m. from a divine sleep by my mother honking her emergency hooter. Was it a robber or a heart attack? I staggered to her bedroom and there she was at the open window, hooting wildly into the night air. She had been driven to the borders of madness by a party raging behind our house and thought, in her crazed, exhausted state, that they might hear her hooter, realise how annoying they were and shut up.

We phoned the Town Hall to alert the Noise Officers, but lucky them, they go home to bed at three a.m. At least my mother sleeps at the back of the house. Stuck at the front I am woken every hour or so by people wandering up and down the street at all hours, carousing, arguing and laughing loudly as if it were lunch-time. I would like to rush out there, hold them up at gun-point and place them in the stocks, gagged, until morning.

Nor can one rest during the day, what with the odd car alarm going off at dawn, thunderous pop music blaring from windows, the house shaken and blasted by passing cars throbbing with noise, Rosemary's Perfect Son practising his drumming and the Daughter and her chums galloping up and down the stairs relentlessly.

And because of the heat we must all have our windows open while the noise of enervated families shrieking within pours out and annoys all the other boiling and exhausted families who are trying to control themselves.

But it isn't just the hot weather. I suspect that the world is growing generally noisier and many of the public are partially deaf. Last night Daughter and I went out to dinner in a restaurant of her choice. Over the thunderous pop music, waitresses shouted cheerfully and Daughter and I lip-read or roared at each other in order to converse. Being one of the new hearing-impaired generation, her ears terminally damaged and senses banged flat by clubbing and very loud music, the Daughter thought this a relaxing venue. Why was I scowling?

We had an uninhibited row about it. Luckily no one could hear us.

The Old Country

My mother and I are off to Hove to visit all the old friends she now never sees and the Crematorium and Garden of Remembrance where my father lies sprinkled round a rose bush.

I have not been looking forward to this trip. The drive is long and exhausting, hordes of friends must be fitted in and I am apt to blub at even the thought of the crematorium and bawl at the sight of a written memorial, even to an unknown cat, never mind my own father. I avoid reading the little plaque under the rose-bush and fiddle about moving the car into the shade, otherwise the dog will expire from the heat and make our day out even more tragic.

My mother is keen to sit in the rose-garden for hours, dead-heading the roses and chatting to the assistant, but we must speed on with our visiting schedule. My mother's friends are thrilled to see her at last and have cancelled their bridge games en masse without a second thought. No other action could so clearly convince my mother of her own worth and their devotion.

The sun blazes down, we sit on sunny patios and flowered balconies, eat a divine lunch, drink tea and hear of all the scandals, bits of bad behaviour and deaths that have occurred since my mother left this sea-side heaven and came to live in stinking London.

Her friend Betty shows my mother the next-door flat. It is empty. It has French windows opening on to Betty's divine

garden and was designed in heaven for my mother. And only
£50 a week!

My mother gazes at it wistfully. It is utterly perfect but two
years too late. If only it had been there when she first thought
of moving, then she would have been in it like a shot, but now
she has grown accustomed to our London hell-hole. It has its
advantages: me, the nearby hospital, the saintly social worker
and her dream-boat doctor. She dare not leave them. Bitter
memories of the South Coast still plague her: the overworked
doctors, insolent receptionists and my father's last grim and
neglected days in the local hospital, our own personal Death
Row. No amount of bridge games, chums and sunny patios can
dispel the terror of this final threat. Our house is now her
home – for better or worse.

Off the Rails

Once upon a time, if you wanted to go on a train journey, you could ring the station, talk to a person, ask for train times and they would look them up in a timetable (in book form) and give you an answer. Now there is a great blockage at the centre of the railway system, like a giant spider, catching the customers in a web and keeping them stuck there, unanswered, until they give up and die. It is called the National Rail Enquiry Bureau.

So it came as something of a shock to me when I rang and was answered by a pleasant fellow almost immediately. He searched for the train times on his computer. Time passed. The man apologised. His computer couldn't find the answers. Slowly it dredged up one train time. More time passed. More apologies. Computer went on searching unsuccessfully for train times to Cornwall.

Perhaps Operator could find out the cost while we waited for the times? No. Computer could only do one thing at once. We waited. Operator sensibly gave up and looked in a book. He found the journey time *and* the telephone booking number.

This number is the blockage supreme and engaged forever. No wonder Telephone Rage is on the increase. The customer must give up trying, go to the station in person and purchase the ticket there. I did, joining a long queue of bad-tempered customers who had also trekked there after being caught in the spider's web. It was eight-twenty p.m. The ticket office closed at nine p.m. Would we get there in time? Customers were on ten-terhooks and rumbling with Queue Rage. I made it, but couldn't buy a bargain ticket, booked in advance, because you had to know the return time, and you couldn't because the timetable would change on August 31st and no one knew the return times until the new timetable came out, so no one could book returns until then, by which time it would be too late to buy advance bargain tickets.

Meanwhile Olga has discovered a direct number to a particular bit of railway selling the ticket she wanted. She rang the National number back in a fury asking why they'd kept it secret. It wasn't their job to sell tickets, they told her, only to give information. It is difficult to know whether things are improving or not.

Old Bulls

What a delightful piece of luck for me to be off for a week's work in the South of France. No household chores, no shopping, no cooking, no mother, daughter or dog for seven days, only Provençale dinners, wine and grown-ups.

This taste of paradise was marred only by our works outing to a bull farm. It is difficult to enjoy one's dinner when the restaurant adjoins Death Row. And it was raining heavily. There, out in the fields and enclosures, were numerous glum black bulls, moaning and roaring with temper and misery, awaiting a brutal death in the ring. The older ones, all ready to die and trained to be bad-tempered, made the most noise, probably because they knew what was coming. Mangy, elderly farm dogs staggered about the barns, the cockerel had a poorly foot and a generally desolate mood pervaded the venue.

Back in the dining room we ate our divine meal surrounded by the odd instrument of torture and boldly coloured pictures of fighting and dying bulls, dripping with blood. The chap next to me turned pale green and was unable to eat his paella. Blinded by migraine, he sat in the darkened coach with a cardigan over his face, while outside the bulls moaned, the giant frogs screamed and the rain drizzled on relentlessly.

Sometimes it is ghastly to be an older male, even if one is not a bull. On returning to our hotel the chat turned to death, disease and the fate of men. They die earlier than women, crash more cars, go bald, are fearfully depressed, commit suicide in droves, their sperm counts are dropping, prostate and testicular cancer are on the increase, and I suspect that men are more prone to piles and pot-bellies. And, says one of my colleagues in France, men also have breast cancer. And their driving deteriorates. My father, driving to the last, would set off from the kerb-side like a maddened kangaroo, my mother screaming with fright beside him.

Back home again a male chum of fifty-four tells me that he now has only a vestigial sex life. Things could be worse. He could have a bald head and a pony-tail.

Boyfriends

It is sometimes difficult for a mother to appreciate the qualities of her daughter's friends, especially if they are male. My daughter and I are visited by chaps, but they rarely come up to my mother's standards.

'There must be something nice about him if *you say so*,' says she bitterly. 'I'd better not say anything. *I might say too much.*' She has occasionally refrained from overt criticism, and she will allow my visiting chap only a small portion of cheesecake. Daughter's boyfriend was allowed none at all. There are ways and ways of expressing an opinion.

Some mothers, even though they loathe these fellows, are able to conceal their feelings, but my mother cannot. Try as she might, waves of hatred swirl about the house, her revulsion is suppressed, but for how long? Often hints of it seep out – a tiny barbed remark, a sulk, a Rosa Klebb look. These are warning rumbles before the explosion of murderous criticism that usually erupts in the kitchen, epicentre of conflict.

Naturally a mother wishes to protect her child from scoundrels and advantage-takers. My mother can spot one a mile off. So zealous is she that sometimes the innocent are falsely accused. Yesterday Rosemary came over for a spoonful of mayonnaise and my mother flashed onto red alert. Unknown to her I had borrowed Rosemary's eggs earlier that day.

'I'd like you to know that this is reciprocal!' cried Rosemary, deeply offended. But usually there is no trial or opportunity for

defence. My mother does not take prisoners. One mis-
demeanour, one helping of ice-cream too many, one lot of
washing-up not done, then the culprit is judged, condemned
and never forgiven. Daughters friend helped himself to toast
without asking, my friend grabbed for extra chocolate cake,
and now it is all over for them.

This does not help when one is trying to conduct a romance,
but my mother has been trained from infancy to be on the
lookout for spongers. Her own mother fought tooth and nail to
banish my father, but fortunately failed. Still my mother presses
on.

'Please Rosemary,' she begged poignantly, 'grant me this one
wish as a dying woman!'

'Of course!' said Rosemary in a fright. 'Whatever is it?'

'DON'T LET HER MARRY HIM!' What a burden for Rosemary!
Only she could save my mother from the eternal torment of
knowing that a parasite may deprive me of all my worldly
goods. And I thought you could stop worrying about daughters
straight after A levels.

Elderly Flesh

It is my birthday and my skin is now fifty-five years old. It is showing signs of decay. Last week I fell into a ditch while picking blackberries and sprained my ankle. It turned into a purple puffball with an egg on the side.

Rosemary's sister, who is a nurse, examined it bravely when she had barely finished her lunch. 'Look!' said she brightly, prodding at it. 'You have pitted oedema!' Each little prod left a yellow pit in the fat.

'What's that?'

'It's what happens to elderly flesh,' said the Sister cheerily. 'It loses its elasticity.' This isn't the only physical defect that a friend has pointed out. Only recently I was out in my sun-top having a coffee with my friend Janet when she suddenly stared at my chest.

'What's that?' she cried, trying to control her revulsion. She had spotted a senile wart. Luckily only one was visible. Unknown to her and concealed by the sun-top, whole clusters of the ghastly things have grown. They were first spotted twenty-five years ago at an ILEA medical.

'Don't get upset,' said the doctor, 'but they're called senile warts.' And I was only thirty. The relentless decline had already started. Now, what with the sprain, angina and arthritis, my mother and I have had a grim week staggering around doing the catering.

Last night, having blundered round the park on crutches taking my dog for a walkie, I returned and sank to the floor, moaning in a dramatic way and unable to move. From there I crawled heroically to the sofa. Meanwhile my mother tottered about the kitchen preparing dinner, and with a superhuman effort, lumbered to the living room with a tray. Immediately she collapsed on her armchair, her face drained of all colour and gasping for breath.

I imagine this scenario reenacted in homes all over the country when the baby-boomers reach their eighties and their meagre supply of children can scarcely help them. Then where will we be?

Luckily Rosemary returned from her holiday and became chief shopper, chauffeur and assistant caterer. What luck that she had postponed her varicose vein operation until October, otherwise we should all three have been shambling about on crutches, a taste of what is to come.

Daughter, meanwhile, phones from Cornwall. She too has sprained her ankle. She sprayed it briskly with medicine and carried on surfing. Just occasionally I long to be eighteen again.

Cripplegate

I am still hobbling around in a sock, scarcely recovered from my horrible sprained ankle, when Rosemary falls down the stairs and breaks hers. We are going down like ninepins over here, the house littered with crutches and our elderly limbs snapping like twigs. There is Rosemary sitting on the stairs holding up her oddly shaped purple ankle. She cannot even bear to dangle it.

Off we all go to hospital. It is like a war zone, flooded with spilt coffee, injured persons sprawling about and a pale lady, possibly homeless, with tatty hair and mottled legs, stuck blankly in a wheelchair. Emergencies have been flooding in and waiting time is six hours.

Still Rosemary is polite and stoical. 'Poor girl,' says she, looking at the exhausted and overworked nurse. 'This is no longer a rewarding job.' Rosemary's daughter and I leave her here in hell where she waits until four a.m. to have her leg plastered, unsuccessfully and without a painkiller. There are not enough staff to supervise it. Next day she must have an operation.

But has she told them of her sleep apnoea? No. I order her to do so. One can take stoicism too far. Suppose her throat closes up mid-op? I am desperate not to have another funeral in our street. Death is creeping nearer and starting to nibble at my friends and acquaintances, and during Rosemary's overnight wait, necrotising fasciitis gobbled someone up in the hospital.

I visit Rosemary after her operation. Her leg looks a fright, and the other one, the 'jealous leg', is covered in a chic white elastic stocking, *and* she has a non-slip bootee and exercise strip. I am rather envious. Trust her to go one better than me and be cosseted, but she was polite to hospital staff, whereas I had a tantrum after a mere four-hour wait with my sprained ankle. We have a desperate and bitter laugh about it. Rosemary grows more serene with age, while I grow more obnoxious. But here is a chance for me to be pleasant. I can now do Rosemary's shopping and chauffeuring for three months, helped by her two saintly children.

This drama has terrified my mother. 'This is Cripplegate,' she cries, and glues herself to the phone warning her friends not to hurry downstairs with the ironing board, as Rosemary did. She watches my movements like a hawk. 'Make sure you have a hand free!' she screams. 'Hold on to the banisters!' Who says the elderly have dull lives?

Retirement Plans

Now that we are all growing feeble and falling about breaking and damaging limbs, our out-of-town retirement colony for the elderly is all the more vital. But where is it to be? Olivia has completely ruled out Gloucestershire. The very rich have moved in and spoilt it, says she. Hedges round the houses are now six foot high, big gates with balls on columns have been erected, mammoth conservatories clamped onto the sides of cottages and every other car is a horse-box. This summer her visit to the favourite pub was marred by elderly persons in shorts carrying rucksacks and exposing their legs. Olivia criticised them harshly.

I am already annoyed with Olivia about shorts. A year or so ago she threw away a divine pair which I longed for and which fitted me to a tee.

'I did you a favour,' said she strictly, and reminded me of my overhanging knee fat. This is not what one expects from friends. How are we to live harmoniously together? And Rosemary is opposed to my dog. Should we share a large, rambling property, it might bounce into her part and frighten her cat. She also objects to some of our partners.

'You can't have *him* in the house,' says she, horrified. 'He'll have to live in a shed in the garden.' And she is now determined on Cornwall. Without consulting anyone else, she has been down there searching for premises. She decided this following a visit to chums in the Home Counties where fresh produce is no longer available. It has all been whipped off to town while yellowing vegetables moulder in village stores, and everyone votes Conservative. These are harsh generalisations but Rosemary is adamant. Only Cornwall will do.

Our commune is obviously going to be difficult to manage with us all squabbling over the location and criticising each others' partners, pets and legs, but I am still keen on it. A financial adviser has just looked into my earnings and savings and he predicts that the minute I retire they will plummet and I shall be on the breadline. If our plans fail I shall be shunted into a 'care warehouse' to sit in a dull armchair and eat sausage rolls for tea, my dog will be banned and I shall never have a horse. It's our commune or the streets.

Memory Lane

Over by London Bridge is a bleak area dotted with warehouses and bridges, tunnels and small mazes of streets. It has recently been discovered by a few elderly artists. What could suit them better than huge spaces at low prices? So they've bought some warehouses and turned them into personal museums, shrines to themselves, continual retrospectives. *And* they all go to the same yoga class. A colony for the talented elderly seems to be springing up over there.

Olga joined the yoga class and heard all about it. 'Mad isn't it?' says she, but being an artist herself she knows that to be a success you need to be completely driven and self-obsessed. Anyway, if one has a vast backlog of charming works, why not put them on display, rather than stuff them away in some old cupboard? Then people can visit, gaze and shop all at once.

Even if you are not an artist, a museum could be useful. I rather fancy one myself. Then I could at least keep a grip on the distant past while my short-term memory cracks up and makes a shambles of the present. This weakness has just lost me my fourth car radio.

My third one had a removable front, but thieves stole the back anyway, even though I had carefully taken the front indoors, so this time I bought a car alarm as well. This should have been foolproof, but for my memory. I forgot to remove the radio front and switch the alarm on. Arriving home late, I rushed in and out of the house and went off somewhere else on foot. The short-term memory, feeling harassed, gave up the ghost and meandered off somewhere. It cannot cope with more than one thing at a time.

Now I notice that huge tracts of my long-term memory are also missing. Someone talks of a major past event in my life – a whole holiday, a romance – and it's the first I've heard of it. I obviously need a museum before everything floats away. I am not alone. Rosemary tells me that a lady peer in the House of Lords recently declared that everyone she had ever slept with was dead. 'What about me?' asked an elderly gentleman present at the time. Who was this poor man, so heartlessly forgotten? Rosemary cannot remember. We are both off to London Bridge.

Crutches

Rosemary is having a ghastly time with her multiply fractured leg and crutches. She absolutely will not listen to advice. I thought we might have a problem after visiting her in hospital. Rosemary hurled her disposable sick bowl across the ward in temper, just because I sensibly suggested she have it nearby.

'Get it out of my sight,' bellowed Rosemary, and threw it. What luck that it was empty! Now she is at home and being disobedient with her crutches. After decades of independence and being in charge, she is not keen on obeying instructions, even from one who has experience. Having learnt all about crutches with my sprained ankle I try to demonstrate their use, but Rosemary flings them to the ground and grabs for the cigarettes. She cannot get the hang of them and stands wobbling about screaming for her Zimmer frame. Yesterday she cried with fright on the pavement, marooned with the dread crutches.

I have had to stop giving robust orders and be sensitive. Rosemary must be allowed to dither about and shuffle along on her bottom without being harassed. The tiniest shopping trip now takes several hours.

Luckily Rosemary's home is filling up with equipment: two wheelchairs (one self-propelling), Zimmer frame, commode and two wheeled office chairs on which she can whirl and twizzle about the kitchen and living room. This has been a gruelling few days for us, as Rosemary rejects the useful advice or gadget when it is given, then, after I've gone home, she tries it and is grateful in secret.

'Try this useful bag,' I shout. 'Put it over your shoulder, carry all essential items in it: cigarettes, lighter, slippers, newspaper, cordless phone, pills.'

'No,' yells Rosemary. 'Take the stupid thing away!'

Later that day she telephones with the thrilling news. 'I love the bag,' she shouts. 'It's very useful.' This morning she used her crutches to rise from her chair, just how I showed her last week. 'It's brilliant,' she roared, 'watch this,' and rose effortlessly.

This must be a foretaste of what is to come, when we are creaking about, old, crippled and stuck in our commune together. We are now prepared for pig-headed behaviour, intransigence and bossiness when one of us in incapacitated.

And now I have a cold. 'It's not a real cold,' says Rosemary strictly. 'It's a demand for attention. You may have *one* day off.'

A saint's life is not an easy one.

Football Season

Striding over the chilly Heath with the dogs, Sylvia and I notice that autumn is definitely here again. It fills Sylvia with gloom. Other people admire the colours of the leaves and the crispness in the air. I rather like the smell. 'What is it?' I ask.

'Decay,' snaps Sylvia, tramping through the mud. She hates the cold and doctors have been coming at her with needles, longing to give her a flu jab, but she has fought them off. And worst of all, autumn is the football season.

This has blighted our home. *Coronation Street* is repeatedly dislodged and my mother is in a fury. 'Bloody football,' she screams, as another evening is thrown into chaos. Meanwhile downstairs the Gardener sits entranced and inert for hours glaring at the telly, a dull and infuriating visitor. I am only cheered by the familiar seasonal sound of the thwacking of police batons on hooligans.

In my friend Olivia's house autumn is also dreary time, the air thick with the smell of unwashed kit and damp leather footballs. On match evenings Husband will slip away from dinner pretending to go to the lavatory, but really he's sneaked upstairs for a shot of football. On Saturdays he hovers all day in front of the teletext, checking the results, his eyes filling with tears if the favoured team loses, his mood grim for the whole day.

Last week Olivia inadvertently overheard a telephone conversation between her Son and a chum. Excitedly she listened in, expecting to hear wild stories of sex and drugs, but no! It was only football.

'Do you think they'll make a transfer?' droned the friend.

'He'll cost about a million,' replied Son. There were long pauses while they breathed quietly, thinking about goals and teams, then the odd, plain remark. Olivia lost interest. She is depressed by this development. When she was young in the Sixties, young men wore velvet jackets, talked about Timothy Leary and Baudelaire, and kept quiet about their love of football, but now they are older and duller, they flaunt it. Gardener has no shame and views it as an art form. He has no team, he never cries, but only stares. In his youth he had better things to do, like conversing and moving about, but now, in the autumn of his life, he wallows in football. I pray he will return to life in the spring.

Empty Nest

We are now well into the Gap Year, Daughter is planning her adventures and for me the Empty Nest looms. My friend Olivia has already had a taste of it. Her son has gone already, off to university.

'I write him postcards every day,' says she poignantly. 'Just Mummy's little thoughts, but he hasn't answered. It's whistling in the wind.' Last week her husband whizzed off to visit the son and came back with a bleak report.

'Your postcards are not all propped up on the mantelpiece,' said he rather callously. Personally he had a thrilling visit, rowing on the river and bonding with the son, while all around them Amazonian girls rowed up and down and exercised fiercely on the banks. Meanwhile Olivia wanders about her silent house, wondering and worrying.

Now it is my turn. Daughter is soon off to Australia with her chum Jennifer from over the road. At least Australia is not a war zone. We plan the tickets and itinerary over coffee at Jennifer's house.

'Australia has more poisonous snakes than anywhere else on earth,' says Jennifer's mother cheerily. She affects an air of care-free enthusiasm but has secretly ground her teeth down to stumps. 'And watch out when the shark flags are up.' Her friends and relatives down-under have described life on the other side of the world: Koala bears are fearfully crabby, gigantic spiders scrabble about, ceilings and countryside are swathed in webs, the tropic sun will roast the Daughter alive and before she even gets there she'll have to go up in an aeroplane.

I have never liked this. Standing at the airport you can look up at the distant silver speck in the sky and think, 'There is my child, millions of feet above my head. Will the aeroplane stay up there?' At our time of life, after the hurly-burly of children and teenagers, we hoped to enjoy the Empty Nest, but it is marred by terror.

When I left home at twenty-one, my mother paced about my empty room weeping, and I had only gone up the Piccadilly Line to Cockfosters. I went to college daily and returned every night to drear lodgings with another female student, where boiled potatoes were served every night for a year by a dull landlady beneath a cuckoo-clock. And my mother was still frightened. She didn't know her luck.

Crutches 2

Weeks have passed and still Rosemary has not got the hang of her crutches and avoids physiotherapy. 'Come and look,' she shouts, 'one leg is withered and the other's like a tree-trunk!' She has taken to gazing at her withered limb and stroking it lovingly. She is a fearfully annoying patient.

Off we went again to the charming nurses at our Health Centre so they could attend to the suppurating leg and hopefully give Rosemary a telling-off. We had a little squabble in the waiting room as Rosemary doddered about on her crutches and I heartlessly ordered her to hurry up.

'Shut up and get me a ticket,' roared Rosemary, lashing out with a crutch. The other waiting patients were thrilled by our spat. There is nothing better, when one is stuck for hours in a doctor's waiting room, than to be diverted by other patients behaving badly, especially if they are mature grown-ups and meant to know better.

'What about a hot chocolate?' I asked Rosemary, trying to be pleasant, but the drinks machine was broken.

'You said that on purpose,' she snapped, 'just so I'd be disappointed.'

Just in time the Nurse arrived. 'Give her a crutch lesson,' I shouted. 'She will *not* do as she's told!'

'She's doing very nicely,' said the Nurse and led Rosemary away to be pampered. But Rosemary and I made up on the way home. We always do. My mother is sick to death of it.

'You're always at *her* house,' she barks. 'Why don't you two get married?' Yesterday she suspected that I had been visiting Rosemary even before making the breakfast. There was my mother, lying in bed starving, and me off negligently playing with my friend next door, but she was wrong. I had been innocently walking the dog.

Naturally Rosemary tried to appease my mother by giving her the Zimmer frame, a real sacrifice considering her difficulty with the crutches, but my mother rejected it out of hand.

'It's no bloody good to me,' she shouted. 'It hasn't got wheels.'

Then Rosemary swapped her car for an automatic and drove my mother all the way to her bridge game, so that I could relax at home. It made her leg throb terribly and me feel guilty, but it was worth it. It silenced my mother for days, so that Rosemary and I could squabble freely.

Ride and Prejudice

My friend Shirley in the North has a new horse. Her last beloved horse died and she has now adopted another rather wild one which bucks and prances about, but she still loves riding and feels tremendously fit. Her horse magazine tells her that the elderly are taking up riding in droves, so why don't I do it? She remembers me as a fairly accomplished girl rider of eleven.

What a good idea. Off I went for a ride last week with the young daughter of a friend of mine. Now I remember why I rarely do this. It is enormously expensive, miles away, costs an arm and a leg and causes pain. And the Instructress was thirty years younger than me. They always are. She saw at once that she had a sack of potatoes up on the horse and naturally issued lots of instructions. She didn't realise that I was only rusty rather than terminally inadequate, and spoke as if to a dim child of ten on her first pony ride.

We were only allowed to walk round the ring indoors. Round and round. My legs, my arms, the reins, and my whole body were all wrong, I was looking in the wrong direction *and* being too kind to my horse. If I was very good, I might, after thirty minutes of strict instruction indoors, walk round a field. 'Can you do a rising trot?' asked the Instructress kindly.

It is horrid, when one is fifty-five, to have someone of twenty point out your failings, especially as, when I was ten, I galloped freely through the New Forest and over the Yorkshire Dales knowing all about reins, technique and posture, but methods have changed, my muscles have wasted away and the horse knew it had a silly on its back. It plodded along, it stopped for grass snacks, it kicked its friend and a young instructress can only judge what she sees.

'Make sure you tell her what you want to do,' my friend Shirley had warned me, but when you are hot, sweating, exhausted, look foolish and your bum hurts, it is difficult to be assertive.

At least I had some lovely new jodhpurs. I rushed next door to show them to Rosemary.

'Take them off!' she shouted in a mocking way. 'You look like a spider!' I dare not show her my hat, whip and boots. My riding dream is shattered. Or is it?

Married Men

My friend Irene, herself divorced, has recently been involved with a married man. She hasn't seen much of this fellow, just the odd evening meal on his houseboat, but being fifty-four, Irene felt grateful for these little crumbs of romance and excitement, even if the weeks and months between them were filled with doubt, guilt, jealousy and turmoil. But now she has suddenly galvanised herself and dismissed this fellow. The crumbs were not worth it.

She is only slightly cheered to know that this is a common problem. Mrs X had a similar affair with an eminent barrister. He had led a sheltered life, married young and never had a misspent youth. Instead he was having a misspent middle age, prancing from woman to woman and leaving a trail of wreckage in his wake.

Luckily Mrs X had a mole in his chambers who was able to report back on his infidelities. The mole noticed that he would doodle the initials of the current amour on his blotter, then in the afternoons he would pace his room in a restless and abstracted way, humming to himself and unable to concentrate when spoken to. Then he would suddenly rush from chambers, presumably to visit the woman on the blotter. Naturally, Mrs X gave him a telling-off.

'Can you substantiate that allegation?' he shouted, quite forgetting that he was not in court, and his affair with Mrs X came to an end. She now has less faith in the judiciary. At least he was only one of many. Rosemary and I have noticed that numerous politicians, doctors, clergymen, academics and judges tend to go on the rampage at this age. Rosemary blames a rigid upbringing at boys' school.

'But why don't they burst out when they leave school and go to university?'

'They're still far too inhibited and wet,' says Rosemary strictly. 'Then some lovely woman takes pity on them, marries them, trains them up a bit, and when she's spent the best part of her life on the project, they bugger off.' There's a sort of flurry of it at this age, she feels, then they all settle down into strokes and senile dementia.

'No wonder English woman have to be so strong,' says Rosemary, looking rather noble. Luckily her husband used to stay at home sulking. It annoyed her tremendously at the time. Unfortunately, it is not always easy to tell when one is well off.

Phantom Pregnancy

Olivia, now in her mid-forties, recently visited an elderly woman artist. As Olivia leaned over to admire the art work, the artist noticed what she thought was Olivia's condition.

'Oh my dear!' she cried. 'You're pregnant and I'm making you stand up.'

This reminded Olivia of a similar observation made by my mother some months ago.

'You look four months gone,' my mother cried in her usual forthright way. So when the artist made her comment, 'four' was the figure that sprang to Olivia's mind. She sat down in the kindly proffered chair, and not wanting to embarrass the artist by telling her the truth (that it wasn't a pregnancy but a wodge of fat), replied 'four months.'

The lady artist was thrilled. Olivia hated to disappoint her and began to live the lie. She started, strangely, to feel fragile and pregnant and is now caught in the web of her own deceit. Pretty soon she'll have to have a pretend miscarriage or abortion.

What a pity that the elderly are so outspoken. It causes havoc. They are wrecking self-images right left and centre. In the summer I was out in the sunny park in my T-shirt playing with the dog when a small elderly woman approached and stared at me in a puzzled way.

'Are you a man or a woman?' she asked sharply. It is grim when, just for a few heavenly minutes you forget your body and feel happy, someone comes along and throws your gender into question, especially if you have a fairly large bust. I told Olivia this story, but it made no difference. She is still horribly depressed and longs for a washboard stomach. And although we both feel tragic about our fat, neither of us can quite decide to exercise regularly. Perhaps we don't really care enough. Exercises have to be done day after day, but outspoken elderly women only crop up now and again.

In this one area men seem to be more fortunate. Their chums and elders rarely comment on their figures, but for women the criticism never ends. Yesterday my mother was advised by one of her bridge-playing chums to give up sugar and lose weight. She was incensed. The few hours of pleasure in her week had been ruined. At ninety-one a washboard stomach is no longer even a dream.

Too Many Cooks

Rosemary and I tried to cooperate over the cooking last night. We found each other very annoying.

'I have a wonderful recipe for spare-ribs,' shouted Rosemary excitedly. 'I'm doing it tonight.' What a coincidence. I was also planning spare-ribs with red cabbage, so I asked her for the recipe.

'I'm not telling,' she snapped. 'It won't go with red cabbage.' Naturally I argued and begged for the recipe. If I wish to make my household sick with two conflicting recipes, then that is my affair. Eventually Rosemary gave in. She would cook double-quantity and give me half. What a saint! But then she fell asleep in the afternoon and was late preparing the marinade, which threw our whole schedule out. If my mother's dinner is served later than seven-thirty it plays havoc with her digestion and she will be up half the night moaning with pain and Rosemary will become a hate figure.

I had to wake Rosemary and tell her to get on with it. She was resentful, but knowing what was at stake she carried on, and our dinner was a roaring success, if rather sickly. But this communal cooking was harrowing and does not bode well for our elderly commune. I see now why collectives are difficult to run.

My friend Fielding, who has experienced collective living, tells me that they tend to have purges. 'The majority gangs up against some poor hapless bastard, who is then exiled from the collective.'

This seems to be happening in my mother's bridge circle. At ninety-one, rather impressively, she has just embarked on a new social whirl of bridge afternoons, but unfortunately, has found fault with a fellow bridge-player. This lady *will* criticise my mother's sugar intake and stretches her legs out under the table in a selfish way, leaving no room for anyone else. Naturally my mother gave her a kick and is stirring up discontent among the players. Imagine my mother in charge of a collective.

Rosemary and I are aiming for a rather more laid-back approach. Despite our catering squabble we have not given up the idea, and I personally have my eye on the ruins of Friern Barnet Hospital. It has everything: a main building (with potential for dance hall, jacuzzi and swimming-pool), outlying chalets, and huge grounds for gardening and farming. Anyone arguing over the marinade could be hustled off to a locked ward.

Bad Tidings

This is a grisly Christmas for Rosemary. Her broken leg is riddled with galloping infections and she is stuck in hospital again. And she was planning to go to Cornwall for the festive season. She cannot bear to stay here. Christmas in London reminds her of her late husband. It was his favourite time of year, when he became vibrant and energetic, excitedly making lists, whirling round from bookshop to bookshop searching for exactly the right present for everyone, hand-printing cards, wrapping things and buying gallons of drink. He threw himself into the spirit of it all, behaved perfectly and even liked visitors.

So now Rosemary likes to take her children somewhere else, free of reminders. Instead she is incarcerated in hospital and must endure a ghastly operation and stay here. She will be condemned to her sofa, issuing commands to others, who will be scurrying around getting everything wrong.

'I'll do it!' I volunteer.

'No,' shouts Rosemary, horrified. She imagines my mother and me screaming and sweating (or swearing) over the turkey and my dog dribbling at the food and terrifying her cat. We shall squabble, our children may not be pleasant to each other and anyway, she wants to make her own lovely bread-sauce and brandy-butter. And her present-opening rituals will be ruined. Her family open theirs in a civilised way after lunch. We tend to tear ours open at dawn.

I am disappointed that Rosemary has so little faith and is so ungrateful. She is also threatening to escape from hospital for a Last Meal. 'You're to come and take me home for fish and chips,' she says bossily. But I won't. I am frightened the leg will get worse and we shall have Long Joan Silver for a neighbour. The most I will agree to is smuggling in some crisps and a weak aperitif.

Naturally, Rosemary is desperate for a stiff drink and some ciggies. No wonder her health is poor. But who can blame her? She is scared to death of another operation on her poor swollen leg. Chilling phrases like 'Avoid the infection reaching the bone' have made us all feel rather shaky AND Rosemary must face Christmas at home without HIM. Next person who sings ''Tis the season to be jolly' gets a punch in the chops.

Through the Nose

My mother's friend Esther is very poorly and in a divine nursing home. I find both of them chatting in the luxurious open-plan lounge when I call to collect my mother. It looks a tremendous improvement on the last nursing home in which they stayed, and no wonder. This one costs well over £100 per day, or presumably over £900 per week. The other was obviously a snip at £500 a week.

Where are these enormous barrowloads of money meant to come from? Luckily for Esther her local council is paying the bulk of the cost. Our council wouldn't do that (my mother enquired immediately just in case they have a few hundred thousand pounds to fling about) and who can blame them? Half a dozen sick pensioners and they'd be bankrupted in no time.

Obviously it does not do to be ill when you're old. I hate to harp on about this, but it does seem horribly unfair. If you're young the NHS pays, but if you're old, *you* pay. If only one could suddenly drop dead at will before one's savings are guzzled up by a nursing home proprietor. At the current weedy rate of nurses' pay, £900 a week would pay for three and a half top-grade qualified nurses, so one wonders where the money goes.

Perhaps it's being spent on delicious and nourishing meals. I hear that this is a frightful problem in the 'cheaper' nursing homes. A gentleman wrote to me in despair about the grim meals that his late father was forced to endure. His mother still remembers by heart the ghastly details of the menu that her husband was invariably offered for his Saturday evening meals.

'And what would you like Mr Stanway? A toasted tea-cake or a corned-beef sandwich?'

Meanwhile my friend Anne is searching for a home for her mother-in-law. She has thoroughly investigated every place for the Elderly Mentally Infirm in Liverpool. Some were grim, but some heavenly, including outings to the Strand, the pub and two weeks in Blackpool to see the lights, all for £240 a week! Unfortunately, Mother-in-Law prefers to stay at home smoking 40 cigarettes a day, wobbling about with kettles full of scalding water and leaving her door on the latch so that robbers can pour in unimpeded. Down here in London the robbers are far more ambitious. They run nursing homes.

Seasonal Bad Behaviour

Something about the festive season seems to make people rather fierce and reckless. Rosemary insisted on staggering down to Cornwall with her broken leg and my mother has been in a temper ever since I dragged the tree in from the garden. I cannot think why. It smelled divine, Daughter decorated it tastefully, it shimmered with delicate baubles and looked like magic, but my mother raged on: '!**!* !**!ing Christmas!'

Then the Daughter announced that she didn't like turkey. She was desperate for duck. Only duck would do. I ran to the butcher to cancel the turkey. Butcher was enraged.

'No Michele,' he roared, drowning in turkeys. 'You can't do that!' I had to lug the turkey home and cram it in the freezer. It's still there. At least my mother should have been pleased. For the first time in sixty years she didn't have to exhaust and sicken herself making the stuffing. But no. She was still in a bitter mood.

'There's *someone else* who wants turkey,' said she petulantly, and pointed to the dog. Meanwhile, Angela down the road had kidnapped Rosemary's cat. Along came one of the daughters to take it down to Cornwall, but where was it? We suspected Angela. She often lures it into her house with snacks and pretends that Rosemary is neglecting it. It was found lingering on Angela's doorstep and whizzed to Paddington Station in the nick of time.

Down in Cornwall Rosemary was faced with another domineering butcher, who bossed the Son into buying a huge turkey. Only the most fiercely assertive vegetarian Daughter could force him to sell them a smaller one. And people have been abusing their bodies right, left and centre. On Christmas Eve in the local pub, Rosemary spotted eight farmers rebelliously eating mammoth T-bone steaks ON THE BONE, with chips, followed by giant ice-cream sundaes. They started off rowdy but went strangely quiet and red-faced at the arrival of the sundaes. Still they ate on. Meanwhile, up in town, my friend, the gardener woke up at dawn, and before he'd scarcely opened his eyes or even had a sip of tea, ate nine chocolates in one go.

And I am still allergic to 'Auld Lang Syne'. It definitely gives me asthma. So I hid in the larder and ate cold pudding until it was over. Thank heavens January is a dull month.

Modern Art

Rosemary and I are fed up with conceptual art: policemen who aren't policemen, fried eggs, floating anuses, corpses and blobs of excrement. She prefers sixteenth-century Dutch interiors and I prefer to gaze at my dog and the Impressionists.

Luckily I can ignore the Art World, but Rosemary cannot. Her family is embroiled in it. Both her daughters and several of their contemporaries have endured art school. At eighteen they were put into white cubicles, 'their own spaces', and told to produce art. One student put a mattress in a skip and got a First, many others, including one of Rosemary's daughters, sank into depression.

They had no drawing lessons and were desperate for a smidgen of guidance or structure, but teachers were rather thin on the ground, mostly busy in distant warehouses and squeezing in the odd day lecturing at art college. As finances are tight in this area, the poor teachers were forced to be somewhat stingy with their time and could spare only the odd minute or two a week to each pupil.

Now Rosemary's son has begun to taunt her with the terrifying words *foundation course*. They send her into paroxysms of fright. For a few fleeting moments she fears that the last and youngest of her children is off to art school, where he too will float away into a limbo of blank rooms and self-motivation. But then he laughs reassuringly and says 'molecular biology' or 'classics' and Rosemary breathes again.

215

Even my own daughter has been considering art school. I told Olga, who teaches in one, and she looked sick.

'No,' she groaned, 'don't let her go!'

I was surprised by Olga's response. I went to art school in my youth and it was heaven. We had a packed timetable, crowds of teachers and fairly constant supervision. But things are different now, says Olga. An art school is not the cosy establishment that I remember. It is a warehouse teeming with unattended students. A teacher may manage to attend to the very talented or very bad, while the middling must just get on with it. No wonder artists grow up to throw shit at the canvas and tend to be petulant and offensive. Perhaps their efforts could be called something else other than ART; VISUAL COMMENT might be more fitting. Then next time we go to an exhibition, we won't be disappointed.

Blankout

I have until now taken the occasional loss of memory in a light-hearted way, but on Saturday the brain took a worrying lurch downhill. There I was, out shopping and wanting to buy some navel oranges. But I couldn't remember what they were called. So I stood gazing blankly at the shop assistant.

'Aa – aar – ah . . .' Nothing happened. No words came out.

'What would you like madam?'

'Aa – er . . .' A broken sound. The jaw hung slackly. I pointed at the citrus fruits.

Assistant had a guess. 'Grapefruit?' No. 'Lemons?' No. 'Clementines?' No. I searched for the word but my brain was empty. I dredged up a little thought. The navel is in the stomach. I moved a wavering hand towards my stomach. Luckily this was a sensitive organic shop where staff and customers are patient with lunatics. At last Assistant guessed right. I bought my oranges.

I had noticed something wrong as I left the house. When I looked at objects, half of them disappeared and a misty area of silver squiggles appeared instead. Now the squiggles had gone, but so had the vocabulary. Perhaps I needed a snack. I doddered over to the baker's wanting a samosa, but couldn't remember its name, nor the word 'triangular'.

I opened my mouth again. 'Aaa . . . ah . . .' Baker looked on expectantly, the queue grew longer, so I gave up and pointed to a pie instead.

On to the next greengrocer's, where I sat down on a box and did more pointing, but forgot the name of a third item. I still can't remember what it was. Did I ever buy it? Will I ever know? Naturally, when I got home I needed a lie down and a rather loud cry. But luckily, after a short rest, the memory had returned.

I am obviously on the way out. Next day I described my ordeal to Olivia on our walk. But she didn't even know what a navel orange was. Where had she been all her life? How could she not have seen and wanted navel oranges? They are so delicious. She said it's because she doesn't wear her glasses while out shopping. All produce appears as a blur. In fact she didn't have her glasses on for our walk. It was the dog leading the blind leading the demented. Our commune for the elderly infirm becomes more vital by the day.

Oh Well

Rosemary seems determined to lead a short but defiant life. During the long months of her leg injury, I have nagged her to try homeopathy. She absolutely refuses.

'What about some acupuncture?' I ask as I visit the sick-bed, 'or some Arnica Accident? To help you relax/stop you smoking/help the healing process?'

'Goodbye!' shouts Rosemary rudely. Her experience of alternative medicine has been ruined by one innocuous practitioner who perhaps unwisely played a tape of soothing music during Rosemary's treatment.

'That stupid tinkly music,' snaps Rosemary, in a tense and brittle mood. Meanwhile her circulation is poor, her lungs full of black treacle and her prognosis grim. Still she refuses to regard her body as a temple. 'I won't do it,' she snaps. 'Lying on silly couches, having coffee enemas and befriending tumours.'

If only she would follow Olga's example. Olga is rarely ill, eats only organic vegetables, makes her own bread (even ciabatta), goes for bracing dog-walks in the vilest of weathers, cycles from the NW to the SE of London every week to yoga class and is the picture of health. Now she has gone off to India for three weeks' yoga on the beach while we all fester in the inner city.

Even my mother has opened her mind to alternative treatments. Once a month she crawls half-dead to the acupuncturist/osteopath/homeopath, and every time she strides home a new woman. I take her there a cripple, she rises up and walks, but Rosemary is not convinced.

Daughter and her chums are reckless with their bodies – smoking and drinking heavily, guzzling junk food, living all night, snoozing all day, or staggering to work on no sleep and coming home in a temper, the body-clock in turmoil. But one expects the young to be cavalier with their personal resources. By the time we reach our age, the temple has started to crumble and needs maintenance. I noticed this particularly as I tried on my new woollen designer-label worm dress which the Daughter encouraged me to buy in the sales. There were my undergarments clearly outlined in fat. It pulped over their edges in a tell-tale way.

'What about a step-in panty-girdle,' cried my mother from the last century.

I don't care. Perhaps Rosemary is right after all. Temples can be in any shape or condition. The odd worshipper will usually turn up.

Off to Oz

Daughter is off to Australia with her chum Jennifer, as part of the wretched Gap Year experience, and soon the nest will be empty for three months. These are desperate days in our house: the packing, washing and losing of vital clothes, the shopping, planning, instructions, booking and phoning and faxing Australia, the sleepless nights.

'Can we please have a roast dinner,' asks Daughter with a tragic stare. 'My last proper home-cooked meal.' We cook one but she cannot eat it. She's too upset. Another row with the Boyfriend has dulled her appetite. Row after row erupts, meal after meal is wasted. The emotional uproar takes its toll on my mother.

'She needs a lift home from Finsbury Park,' she roars. 'How's she going to get to bloody Australia? You've *no right* to let her go.' She imagines rampant males, poisonous snakes and robbers queuing up to pounce on her only granddaughter at the other side of the world where we shall be unable to save her.

But Daughter is like a caged lioness. For years she has longed to run away from us and roam about the world and now at last she is going. It is Departure Day. We are up at dawn, off to the airport, reach the check-in, but just our luck – the computers collapse. The airline stops functioning 'world wide', enormous queues form, planes are cancelled, hours pass, the airport is clogged to bursting with passengers until at last, four hours late, off go the Daughter and Jennifer, our lovely girls, all by themselves up into the cloudless blue sky in a 394,620-ton tin can for eighteen hours.

Back at home we pace about, wondering. Have they landed/crashed/missed a connection? The house is silent: no shrieking, no clodding feet up and down the stairs, no banging doors. We spend a strange, half-sleepless night. Three-thirty a.m., the phone rings. It is the Daughter, in Singapore airport. The flight was torture, no room to cross their legs, no sleep. She phones the next day – they have landed. And the next day – she misses us and the Boyfriend. And the next day – will we ring back, send a fax, write a letter? She has now lived for three days away from her Boyfriend and mobile phone, the sun is brutal, the wind fierce, the bedroom full of lizards. Only eleven and a half weeks to go.

Yoga

Olga has returned from her yoga holiday in India in despair. After the tropic sun and silvery beaches of the Bay of Bengal, Kentish Town Road is something of a let-down. And also, the yoga part of her holiday was torture. The Quiet Healing Centre was bitterly disappointing and its residents fairly crotchety. After several years in India, they had all managed not to learn Tamil.

Olga and her friend Hilary spent sleepless nights on thin, lumpy mattresses on wobbly plank floors, divebombed by screaming mosquitoes, and rose at dawn for yoga lessons. But the teacher scarcely noticed them. She attended only to the young, supple and talented pupils, leaving the rest to struggle on alone. Some struggled too hard and injured themselves. Muscles were pulled, nerves trapped, hands went numb. A typhoid-like fever swept through the colony. Olga felt old, stiff and unattractive. Then she did her back in.

'I've hurt my back,' she told the class. They were thrilled.

'Something must have really begun to move,' they chorused knowingly.

Olga replied rather crudely and gave up. Watching the advanced class tying themselves into triple sheep-shanks, she suddenly felt that yoga was a form of madness. Instead she and Hilary went shopping and sightseeing, which was bliss. Then one day, as they were chatting to a lady (in mime) about their children and families, along came a male interpreter. At last the lady could ask a question she'd been longing to ask but couldn't express in mine. 'Were they men or women?'

Naturally Olga and Hilary were rather upset. They'd been observing the dress codes carefully, wearing sleeves and long trousers, not wishing to cause offence or inflame men's passions, while all the time no one had had an inkling what sex they were. It was an easy mistake for them to make. They have short, boyish haircuts, trousers, flattish chests and no make-up, which often puzzles the people of Barrow-in-Furness, never mind Tamil Nadu. I have noticed this when visiting my cousin in the North.

No wonder Olga is fed up. It's February, chilly, she is dissatisfied with her work, her child will soon be leaving the nest, she has reached her fifties and love eludes her.

'I'll be sitting here all alone in my basement, withering away,' says she poignantly. But at least here in North London we all know she's a girl.

Cracking Up

My American Cousin has had a desperate week. Her washer-dryer has broken down, her fridge is faulty, her answerphone won't work, her CD-player bust and her fax-machine ground to a halt. Nothing functioned properly, including her own body. So she went to a lovely concert to perk herself up, but her self divided into two. One side was in heaven listening to the divine music, but the other side kept reminding her that her life was turning to ashes.

'I'm divorced,' said the grim side, 'my son's heading for divorce, my father's in a geriatric rage, his future is behind him, I have a calcified fibroid and attend weekly bladder-control clinic.'

It isn't really wise, when one is feeling fragile in February, a difficult time of year, to plunge into another risk area, but for some mad reason Cousin applied for Call Minder. She was determined to have it. So she spent most of Friday morning shouting Yes and No answers to a pretend robot voice. She spoke to four living persons first, who all gave four different answers to the same question, then the robot questioned her relentlessly. Did she like her message/want it changed/how many pips did she want/what sort?

'YES. NO. NO. YES,' screamed my Cousin. She got into a sort of Pavlovian rut with her screaming. When ordinary people ask her ordinary questions she now shrieks YES and NO loudly and sharply.

Michele Hanson

Meanwhile I too have been fighting bits of equipment. My car needs a new clutch, my fridge door won't shut, my lavatory pipe is dripping, the guttering has cracked and water leaked into the newly painted hall, my cordless phone has broken, no one will mend it and the help-line won't answer.

At least Cousin had a chance to shout, even if it was just Yes and No. In my battle to get the cordless phone repaired I was only instructed to press buttons. 'You have six choices,' said the robot. 'Press 1 for blah, 2 for blah . . .' over and over again. So I screamed to myself as I pressed, my mother stamped about her room, unable to phone her chums, her delicate network of bridge games under threat.

At least Cousin knows she is not the only one fighting appliances. They are driving us both to an early grave. And we bought them to make our lives easier.

Piles

There is a sort of camaraderie among people with piles (if they ever find each other) because THEY KNOW. They recognise the strange, shuffling walk, the expression of constant pain, the slow and anguished sitting down and getting up and the way that life is suddenly drained of all pleasure. And as one grows older, the piles can easily get worse.

I had them once. I tried to carry on with normal life, but suddenly, in the middle of my shopping, I had to give up and fall into a taxi. The driver asked me what the problem was. With piles you may reach a stage when you no longer care who knows, who laughs or who finds you offensive.

'Piles,' I snapped. The driver was most concerned. He was a fellow sufferer. (Long-distant drivers often are.) He leapt from the cab, helped me out with my shopping, and as we were standing there in our odd way talking about our condition, along came a chic young woman with golden flick-ups and an apricot suit, wanting to hail the taxi.

She faltered on the kerb-side, probably sickened by our conversation, but who cares. We had both found sympathy and we needed it. You can't sit, you can't stand, you can't move, and no one cares. Break a leg, have the 'flu, burst an ear-drum or an appendix and you may describe the agony, brandish the wound, moan and cry out, but not with piles. People will mock or say 'Please!' in a pained way.

As I lay in bed after my taxi ride, a grumpy television repair man turned up and told me of a strange cure. 'Find a cobra's skull,' he said fiercely, 'cut it into a ring with glass, NOT METAL.'

Where was I to find one? I asked, sneering faintly.

'If you're going to laugh,' he threatened, deadly serious, but I begged him to continue. 'Put the ring on the little finger of your left hand, and your piles will go in a fortnight.' I never got it together.

Luckily mine disappeared and have not yet returned, but my father spent years in hell and my mother's are growing worse. At least she has broken through taboos and inhibitions and discusses them boldly. In more bitter moments she wishes them upon public figures of whom she disapproves, like a curse. I must take care not to annoy my mother.

Bad Hair Decade

An old chum came to visit whom we hadn't seen for years. He looked ever so well, except for his hair, which had completely vacated the top of his head, leaving a shining bald area. He is tormented when out and about by those horrible videos in stores under halogen lighting. Last week he spotted himself on screen in Dixon's from the back, the huge bare tract of skull gleaming away. In despair, he tried a dangerous ointment. A little hair grew, and then his scalp burst into a scabrous pox and shed storms of dandruff, so he gave up. He is contemplating castration, the only cure left to him.

But my friend Fielding has decided to take an 'I'm bald, I can deal with it' attitude. He has gone for the Bruce Willis, tufty, decisive look. 'Seen from below,' says Fielding, 'it looks as if I've got lots of hair. It may convince diminutive people.' So he's not really that bold. He admits. It's just a last-ditch attempt not to be invisible to women.

Thank goodness he's got rid of the lank wisps now, avoiding a 'comb-across' and before the wisps have hung down round the edge of a bald skull, or worse still, been gathered into a ponytail. What a strange style that is!

Meanwhile I am growing a moustache. This is obviously the time of life when things go haywire for everyone. Men cling to their scraps of hair, and we battle to get rid of ours. Hairs sprout everywhere: out of nostrils, ears, chins and moles. My face has become a shrubbery. Some days my moustache isn't there, some days I see a Mexican bandit in the mirror. If I powder over it, it looks darker and fiercer. Recently the Daughter gave a cry of horror and pointed to my chin. There was a mile-long hair, sprung from nowhere. It is tough for a stylish daughter to have a bearded and moustachioed Mama. So I have appointed her as watchdog. Failing eyesight and memory mean that left to my own devices, I might easily leave the house looking unsightly.

Daughters can be harsh critics. Fielding returned home with his new, tufty hairstyle expecting congratulations, but no.

'You look like a gay squaddie,' cried the daughter. Luckily, my daughter has passed from the critical to the advisory stage. One good thing about growing older – the Daughter is growing older too.

Spring

Spring is here, the almond blossom has come and gone and the frogs have been carrying on in the pond, croaking and squeezing each other en masse. I heard on the radio that they are in 'clusters of sexual frenzy'.

They, at least, are in heaven, but for some of us, spring can be something of a struggle. Gardener and I are exhausted from lugging the frogspawn in and out of the house in buckets to save it from the frost, and outside, cats from the neighbouring gardens gather around our pond, waiting to massacre the lovely froggies.

Over in Sylvia's garden, the grey squirrels have been biting the heads off her camellias and throwing them about the garden. Last year they did it to the pinks. They are hooligans. Her plants must now be fenced in and netted over until the garden looks like Alcatraz.

The poet was right, this is a cruel month. For my mother, still exhausted and enfeebled by winter, with every limb aching, it is galling to watch everyone else prancing about and admiring the spring. And the dog and I have a stomach complaint. I return from the doctor's brandishing a packet of Fybogel. My mother is thrilled and laughs in a mocking way. She has been taking this stuff for years but now here am I catching up fast. Fybogel usually comes along with the bus pass, but mine is early.

Meanwhile my mother and I are in and out of hospitals like a couple of yo-yos. We hear that this is a grim season for patients. It is the time of year when *certain councils* run out of money, so they can't send anyone for tests or treatment for several more weeks until next year's budget starts. Only those who've been waiting nine months already, or urgent cases, may be seen. But how are the poor consultants to know who's urgent until they see them? So they sit twiddling their thumbs, watching the daffodils, waiting for the next financial year and the money and patients to flood in.

At least our forsythia has burst into flower. It hasn't done this for two years, since the Gardener pruned it rather brutally. My mother has never forgiven him for murdering her favourite plant. Now at last, she may relent and behave graciously towards him. We live in hope. Just the right mood for spring.

Outings in the Sad Coat

jumped into a taxi the other day in a fairly stable mood, until the driver asked me a question. 'Are you a teacher?'

'No,' I lied, immediately downcast. Our Government's attempts to change the image of this profession had obviously not filtered down to either of us. There I was in the Daughter's old grey school duffle-coat, my dog-walking shoes and an apologetic demeanour and both the driver and I thought I looked like a teacher. To us, subliminally, a Teacher was a drab and pitiful creature, a spinster governess or low-paid servant to even the grimmest of parents.

I, especially, ought to have known better. From my experience at the gruelling chalk-face, I know that the majority of staff are heroic figures: chic, dynamic, calm, highly skilled and battling stoically with an Everest of work and enormous classes, each with its own sprinkling of young psychotics. I have never seen one in a duffle-coat.

Officially mine is for dog-walking, but sometimes I pretend it won't matter and wear it elsewhere. Last week I wore it on a night out with Olivia and Angela to the Pharmacy – that artistic new restaurant decorated with shelves of dummy medicines. What a mistake. It was full of the young, with spiky greased hair and mobile phones, drinking cocktails under rather harsh lighting. Waiters wore operating gowns and the atmosphere was bleak, brutish and noisy. But the menu was strangely infantilised and Olivia refused a snack. She could have egg and soldiers at home. We stared listlessly at the medicines and sat close to the Fybogel.

Soon Angela began chatting to the fellow next to her. She discovered he was a divorced and wealthy poet from Rome. He drank heavily, ate hamburgers and bought us all a drink. Olivia was in Hell. 'Do you remember going out with friends who started to pick up men,' she whispered, feeling sixteen again and hopeless.

Then the duffle-coat began to work its poison again.

'I think you have been on demonstrations in the Sixties,' said the poet. 'Late Sixties,' he added, to soften the blow. He didn't like to generalise, but he could tell, he said, from my fringe. And, I suspect, from the coat. That was all he had to say to me. He much preferred Angela. Perhaps the coat had put him off. No wonder I am still fond of it.

It is sometimes difficult to cope with modern cultural changes. Sylvia and her chum went to a semi-fringe theatre last week. It was a matinée and the audience was filled with white-haired elderly ladies. An actress once told Sylvia that from the stage, such an audience looks like 'a sea of cauliflowers'. There was rather a bold scene in this play in which an actress sprawls across a sofa, legs apart, with her lover on his knees doing good-ness knows what. What were the Cauliflowers to make of it? In their youth, one didn't do things like that on stage, and possibly not even at home, Sylvia thought. But they all stuck it out bravely, and if they could do that, then Olivia and I could manage the Pharmacy.

Costa del Plastica

Rosemary returns from her short holiday in Spain with a very grim report. At first she stayed in a sea-side hotel while her two friends proceeded up the mountains to a charming cottage they had rented last year. In her hotel, couples sat stolidly at breakfast asking each other if they'd slept well, no one shared tables and Rosemary sat alone. She felt not the slightest shiver of embarrassment. Off went the couples on a coach to Gibraltar, the Rep begging them to bring her back Marmite and chocolate digestives from Marks and Spencer's, while Rosemary paddled in the sea and sat on her balcony, resting her injured leg, drinking G & Ts, reading and gazing at the sunset and feeling only slightly sorry for herself.

For a treat, her friends whisked her up the mountain in their car, but things were not as she remembered them. The scenery had changed dramatically. Where there had once been terraces of olives, almonds and figs, there were only endless fields covered in yellow plastic, dotted with plastic sheet factories guarded by fierce, chained dogs. The plastic covered acres of tasteless flat green beans, which we are told the whole of Europe loves and must have. And tomatoes and giant watery strawberries.

The drive to their cottage was now a kilometre-long rubbish tip and the yellow plastic fields came right up to the borders of their little garden on one side. Through a few chinks, Rosemary spotted the odd tendril or leaf. She and her friends had their

235

divine breakfast looking the other way, at what used to be the view, but through a criss-cross of wires, which would soon support more plastic. Young men balanced cheerily on the wires, adjusting the tension. Rosemary imagined old men eating hunks of cheese while gazing across a vineyard: the timeless, ancient Spain that tourists tend to go for.

Back in her hotel, depressed by her travels, Rosemary wondered whether old bodies ought to be undressed and exposed to the merciless Spanish light. She kept hers strictly covered up. But the holiday has done her some good. Her leg's better, she has more energy and wishes to mix more with the young. The undiluted company of the Over-Sixties, reminiscing, having coach rides, short naps and ice-creams, was more than she could bear. That and the yellow plastic.

Homeward Bound

Last week Daughter rang from New Zealand. 'Quick,' she hissed, 'ring me back!' Naturally I rang at once. Daughter had dreadful ear-ache and was off to hospital. She was in pain, had a cold, was homesick again, her new jumper had disappeared from the youth hostel, which was infested with cockroaches. 'Honestly. This girl found a nest of them in her rucksack after she left.'

'Don't move to the country,' she begged movingly. 'You won't like it. You'll like it for a few weeks, then you'll get bored. Like me.' For years she has longed to go to the other side of the world, but now she's there, she yearns for Holloway, her own home town.

For the first few weeks of her travels, phone-calls, faxes and letters had flooded in. The Nest wasn't really Empty. Daughter was here in voice and spirit. Then the phone-calls thinned out. She had really gone – white-water-rafting, surfing, clubbing and partying, presumably enjoying herself a world away from her Mummy.

No calls for a whole week. Why? Our house was silent. The dog often whimpered in a tragic way. I heard on the news that 300 people a year drown in Australia. We were desperate for her to phone again. The dog and I trailed into Rosemary's kitchen to express our anxieties.

'Don't be so wet,' snapped Rosemary strictly. 'No news is good news.'

Then, after the ear-ache, came a sharp increase in calls, perhaps because the New Zealand weather was dull, although the scenery was stunning. 'But you know me and scenery,' said the Daughter wearily. Scenery has never been a priority for her. She preferred Sydney, where you can party and shop until you drop. And now her shopping money must be wasted on doctors.

Then another red alert – food poisoning in Fiji. The Boyfriend had worked and saved for months, flown to the ends of the earth to meet her, and there they all were, throwing up together. No more news. Were they in paradise? Hell? The mouth of a volcano? And how much of this could we stand?

Meanwhile, here at home we live a spartan life, no cakes, biscuits or chocs, few snacks, healthy bread, tons of greens, the dog continues listless, and upstairs the Daughter's room is strangely immaculate and silent. Only two days left, one long-haul flight and the Daughter will be safely back again. Please.

Dog Days

What has happened to my dog's insurance? I opened my renewal document to find that costs have rocketed. Back in the old days, when the divine creature was a puppy, it cost a snip, around £50. Now that she is old, frail, balding and prone to eye-ulcers and bowel disorders, it has zoomed up to £190, including £15 elderly dog supplement and over £50 for living in London. Why? I ring Pet Plunder and complain. They have recently discovered that vets in London charge more. 'We've only just picked up on that,' said the receptionist brightly.

I am furious. I rush round to the vet with my claim form. But wait! There's a little bit of information I haven't noticed. £100 excess on each separate claim. The dog will have to break all its legs at once before I get a penny back. I drive home in a bate and cancel my policy. Naturally, no other insurance company will take the dog on. Now it will probably develop a vicious disease costing thousands in vet's fees and medicines.

It does so the very next day. Its bowels go haywire, just as Olga and Olivia are here having a sophisticated coffee and croissant before we go for a bracing walk over the Heath, but can we go? The dog is busy vomiting and doing other awful things in the garden. I examine everything. Something is seriously wrong. I have a cry in the kitchen. But the dog still wants its walkie. We take it out for a short stagger but have to turn back. The dog looms about looking desperate.

I take it to the vet and have another cry in the surgery. Is this the beginning of the end? No. It's colitis. The dog recovers, but for how long? Boxers only last about ten years and it is ten and a half. I was wandering about the Heath the next day, thinking about this and weeping to myself, when another dog-owner passed by. Her daughter also has an elderly Boxer and walks about crying. She assures me that I am normal. For a Boxer owner.

What a relief. I return home feeling more cheerful and cast the Reaper to the back of my mind. There is my mother at the kitchen table. 'What if the dog and I die in the same week?' says she while rolling out some pastry.

Vile Bodies

An upsetting moment in the bath for me – as I sat there I noticed that my bosoms were resting on my stomach. The effect was that of a mound of filled balloons. It is helpful to talk about these things, I find, rather than cry quietly in one's room, so when Fielding phoned, I told him about it.

'Were you lying down?' asked Fielding. He has a poor grasp of anatomy. No. I was sitting upright. I remember, for a few worrying weeks last summer, that my frogs looked very similar. They lay about the pond, bloated and looking rather sad. Luckily for them, the condition was only temporary.

Then I told Olga, but she feels that there is nothing wrong with having a few rolls of fat. She doesn't have any, because of all that yoga and cycling, and is still dissatisfied with her bosoms. 'They look like two string bags with a potato in the bottom,' says she, dispirited. And Olivia is fed up with hers because since she began her HRT they have grown enormously, overflowing almost every known brassiere and spreading round to her back. Sometimes, looking down at the various mounds of herself, she feels that there are several other people present. And dieting is pointless. Olivia has tried it in the past, everything shrank except for the bosoms and she ended up looking like a tadpole.

I see now why my mother is preoccupied with her body. At this age one becomes more aware of it, in a somewhat negative way. Miserable little events draw it to your attention. Olga and her friend Anne were looking at their Indian yoga holiday snaps when Olga spotted someone strange.

'Who's that funny old man?' she asked. And just as the words were coming out of her mouth, she realised that it was her. A grim moment for Olga, but she is far from alone. Once, on holiday, I met the most beautiful woman in the world. As she walked along, crowds stood still and gaped, the town stopped breathing. But she hadn't always looked like this. For most of her life, she told me, she'd had a 'bulbous tip' nose. She had it altered and for a few months felt perfect. Then one day she noticed that her bosoms were far too small. It ruined her new-found happiness. There is a message here somewhere.

The Male Brain

This is a dismal time for us. The World Cup is drawing near and already ruining dinner parties. We had one on Saturday and of the four chaps present, three droned relentlessly on about football. Fielding was the worst. He has even sunk to begging the autograph of a famous football person and pretending it was for his daughters. He was shameless and bragged at table.

'HE didn't have to sign it,' said Fielding with reverence, as if personally blessed by Christ, 'but HE did.'

Disappointingly my friends Toad and the Gardener egged him on, and as a tiny sop to the other guests, they made up a literary team: Camus in goal, Keats all over the place, Orwell on the left (or right?) wing, Marlowe as striker.

My visitors were all grown-ups but seem not to have developed. Daughter's male chums, thirty years younger, are behaving in exactly the same way – videoing matches, gawping and roaring at screens. Last night they visited a neighbour and watched videos of three years of Arsenal highlights. Naturally Daughter ran home bored to death, but they followed her and played Nintendo virtual football in our house. Daughter had a scream at the top of the stairs, and who can blame her? We are planning to ban the lot of them from our house for most of the summer.

Olivia is more charitable. 'It's the last area of masculinity left to them,' says she. They have no call-up, little heavy manual labour, they may even be required to do fluffies' work, tidying and babysitting. So all up and down our street young and adult males gather (or sit alone) in their front rooms shouting at tellies.

Perhaps, if the male brain is compartmentalised, there is one very large and dominant compartment full of sport. Other compartments become cramped and impaired, and one of these is the 'how-does-my-obsession-affect-others?' compartment. 'Who cares what girlies think?' it says. 'They're not serious. They may lose their squeaky little tempers and flail their weedy arms about, but they'll get over it.' Wrong. One day, when the World Cup is all over, and a pizza is a pizza again, not a 'half-time snack', Sainsbury's has stopped giving out football medals, and the cover of every publication no longer pictures stump-headed football-playing dumbos, the hateful memories will linger on. It is often difficult to admire, or forgive, a football fan.

It's My Party

On Friday Rosemary was sixty. She and her son spent a glamorous few days in Paris being pampered by chums, while her two saintly daughters stayed at home preparing the birthday party. Rosemary returned to find the house nearly transformed, too many visitors had said yes, there weren't enough chairs, plates, cutlery, space, drinks or food, and then she lost her front tooth. Panic stations. Should she cancel? How can one entertain dozens of smart guests looking like a toothless crone?

'Why are we doing this?' wailed Rosemary, scrabbling through the rubbish-bin searching for her tooth.

And her son was absent, usually a calming influence and reliable wine monitor. He was still in Paris, about to cycle alone across Spain for six weeks on the trail of Laurie Lee, Orwell and the Spanish Civil War. Rosemary was demented with worry about her Boy.

No son, no tooth, the bottle-opener had disappeared *and* my mother and Rosemary's mother had squabbled over their bridge games, so my mother would not go to the party. 'I don't like crowds,' she snaps. 'They make me dizzy.'

Unwisely I suggest she makes Rosemary a birthday strudel.

'No I bloody won't,' she screams. 'I've done the salmon, you've done the *tiramisaloo* and you've been over there all bloody morning!' The air in our street quivers with loathing and tension, like a sort of electric heat haze, and by party-time

245

Rosemary is a wreck, but at least she has found her tooth. It was in her dressing-gown pocket.

I make off through the crush of guests with plate of party lunch for my mother. Rosemary's mother spots me. 'Isn't your mother coming?' she asks politely. No. I nip home again and find my mother groaning in the garden. She has fearful indigestion.

'Aaargh!' she screams with pain. 'This is why I don't like eating in public. Tell Rosemary.'

But Rosemary has other worries. On her way home from Paris she had headed automatically for the duty-free to buy her Boy his usual chocolate, but just as she reached the counter, she realised he wouldn't be home. She was gripped by a terrible empty feeling. It lasted right through into her party, but oddly enough, the party was a roaring success. Rosemary loved it. She just wished for her departed husband and absent son as she blew her candles out.

Hobbies

I am plodding on with my cello practice. To my mind I am improving tremendously and can now play recognisable tunes. And I am more relaxed. I no longer hold my bow in a vice-like death grip, but I admit progress is slow. I am still not bringing joy to people as I play. Even the dog looks rather sullen.

Today I tried a vibrato. Teacher has at last given me permission to do so. For months I have longed to do this. I imagined people swooning with pleasure as they passed by and heard such expressive playing, but they didn't. My vibrato sounded like a hornet in a temper and after a few brief seconds I had a fearful pain in the end of my finger.

In fact both my new hobbies are causing pain. The riding is also gruelling, despite my padded knickers, but I shall plod on. If I can't have a pert, bouncy bottom ever again, perhaps I can have a resilient leathery one. At least Rosemary admires my choice of hobby. She inclines towards gentler pursuits, perhaps some mild gardening. 'And now my leg has gone, I'll never surf,' says she poignantly.

Meanwhile, things are looking up. The asthma, sweating, headaches, exhaustion and battered spine that I once battled with while plodding round the ring are now fading, and I am allowed to go galloping over the Heath. Last week I fell off and foolishly let go of the reins. The horse was thrilled. It frolicked about somewhere around the back of Golders Green, snacking on the lovely green grass and frightening motorists until the other more efficient riders corralled it into a corner.

Thank goodness my mother didn't witness this incident. She tends to he unhelpful when one is struggling with a new skill.

'What a bloody awful row. It sounds like a sick cow!' she roared from her bedroom last week as I played what I thought to be a moving little piece of Purcell. Then she came grinding downstairs on her stairlift and stuck her head round the door looking gloomy.

'D'you think you ought to go on with these lessons? They're not doing you much good,' said she in her forthright way. She has still not quite got the hang of positive reinforcement. Even now.

Rosemary's Baby

Now that Rosemary's birthday is over, she is free to worry desperately about her Boy, off cycling alone across Spain. Every few days the Boy phones from some remote village that Rosemary has never heard of, sometimes missing her and leaving a faint and poignant message on the answerphone.

'Goodbye Mum,' said the voice, sounding oddly tragic, and Rosemary's heart nearly broke. But now she has pulled herself together and bought an enormous map of Spain, pinned it on the kitchen wall and is following his route as he diddles his way down to Seville, living on tinned tuna, a squirty tube of mayonnaise and the odd apple. He pitches his tent all alone, here and there, by a roadside, in a field, an easy prey to any wandering madman. Naturally Rosemary is terrified, especially as her Boy has already written off two bikes in the Holloway Road: one into the back of a bus and one into a stationary car.

Yesterday, as we were trying to have a relaxing drink in the garden, the Boy rang. Rosemary staggered to the phone. 'My Darling Baby Boy,' she cried in a sickening way. Had I said that to my Daughter, she would have mocked cruelly.

'He's just cycled for half an hour through a hail-storm,' wailed Rosemary. 'Poor baby!' Rosemary's boy is a hulking but sensitive fellow of nineteen. 'It's making me more tolerant of your ridiculous behaviour over that dog,' she snaps.

Why the dog? Why not my Daughter? She feels that the dog is closer to death and the level of risk that her Boy is running.

'It's not the empty nest I mind,' says she. 'I don't mind a rest from the ceaseless drumming, the big meat dinners and a large boy loping about, just the terror.'

Meanwhile, our nest is still choc-a-bloc. Sometimes Daughter leaves it to seek a job. She often searches the sunny Heath and parks for employment, sunbathing and picnicking with chums to stave off exhaustion and disappointment. My friend Jim's son is rather less dynamic. He rises at two, breakfasts and sits about during the afternoons, waiting patiently for an employer to sense that he is there, ring up and offer him a well-paid job in a record shop where nobody minds wild dreadlocks and a pierced eye-brow. Lucky Rosemary.

Cable Rage

We were woken at seven a.m. on Friday by loud clangings and bangings, and then at seven-fifty-five a pneumatic drill started up. It was Cable coming to our street. First we'd heard of it. No letters, no discussion, no 'Would you like this amenity in your house?' Just the noise at dawn, the red and white barriers and mud everywhere, nowhere to park and eventually over forty channels of crap on telly.

I know because the Gardener had Cable free for a month. This was a special offer to compensate for them running the cable straight through the middle of his garden twice. He watched it carefully, night after night, channel after channel, and found nothing to his liking except, of course, more sport.

Sylvia already has Cable in her street. She never wanted it. In fact not one single person in her whole street wanted it. Every resident said no, signed petitions, begged for Cable not to be installed, but it was. It is apparently compulsory. Naturally I rang and complained.

'Is it inconvenient?' asked the man on the phone, as if a brand-new thought had just struck him.

Yes. He asked how. This is the sort of occasion on which I long for an omnipotent god to lean down from the sky with giant pincers, pluck the fellow out of his office and place him in my room, close to the pneumatic drill. Or he could sit next to the Gardener and watch him flipping channels. This is a maddening habit, even with only five channels to flip. Gardener flips so quickly that other viewers are only allowed a micro-glimpse at possible choices. I spot one that I want, I scream 'Stop', but Gardener is already three channels ahead. Imagine him with forty to choose from. And Rosemary still hasn't even got to grips with Channel 5. It has somehow passed her by.

Meanwhile the workmen have gone, leaving bits of barrier behind, just to annoy. Junctions and short-cuts for miles around are bunged up with Cable works, and for what? To drive my mother insane? I hear that elderly persons who sit gaping at the telly for hours on end may suffer from delusions, brain damage and memory loss. From her bedroom I hear my mother calling, 'Goodbye Tinky-Winky,' and she only has four channels on her telly. Go away Cable.

Babies

Olga and I were walking the dog when we passed a woman with whom Olga was acquainted. She had two little children with her and a brand-new baby in a sling.

'You've got another one!' shouted Olga laughing cheerily. 'How ghastly!' Then a few steps further on she regretted her comment. When one spots a new baby, the thing to do is rush up, admire it effusively and congratulate the new mother, not recoil and mock.

Olga may be forthright, but I rather agree with her. Last week I spotted a lady out in the park with two toddlers, one weeny baby and a very large Retriever. Little bicycles were strewn about, children and dog striking out in different directions, the baby blubbing and the mother looking worn out with her hair awry. What bliss for me to be playing a relaxing game of football with my old dog. This has to be one of the benefits of being fifty-five: no babies to look after.

Rosemary had one to visit yesterday. It was three and wanted to dig the garden, fall in the pond, torment the cat, spray water and drink juice. Rosemary had no juice. Her home is no longer baby-friendly. She and the mother had to dart about finding spades, defending plants and frogs and whipping up snacks, while in between tasks, its mummy was able to tell Rosemary about the rest of her life, in joined-up sentences.

We are not even keen on the older children. Fierce gangs of them roam our street, yelling, scratching any nice new shiny car, smashing windscreens, pinching radios and terrifying the smaller, more innocent children who play properly on the pavements, making little shops at their gates and wanting to wash cars.

Sometimes, I want nothing to do with children at all. 'Perhaps you never liked them,' says Fielding harshly, in the tone of Witch-Finder General. It is a vile, unnatural thing not to like children. I loved mine of course, even when she was puking and waking up at dawn. But now the cartoons, sandpits, schools, parties, leisure pools, pulling little gloves, socks, shoes on and off are over, I never want to do them again.

So we are dreading the advent of grandchildren. But we have been assured that we will love our own to distraction. We just will. Meanwhile, this is a pleasant interlude.

We've Been Framed

My mother has set her heart on a three-wheel Zimmer frame on which she can scoot along the pavement, rather than the sort she has to pick up and plonk down all the time. The very lovely three-wheel folding ones are available in a big chemist's in central London.

We ring to make sure they have one. 'Yes. We always have one for you to try,' says the Chemist Woman, so off we go, on a Saturday afternoon in the searing heat and get stuck in a 'Reclaim the Streets' traffic jam. Or is it a bomb in Camden? Reports vary. My mother is quaking in her seat. And this was meant to be a pleasant outing. She imagined herself perhaps having delightful tea and cakes at Sagné's in Marylebone Road, a divine patisserie that she remembers from her youth. Instead we are sweltering in traffic.

At last we reach the chemist's. You guessed it. No Zimmer.

'What is Zimmer?' asks a baffled assistant. Another assistant goes to search for one. 'Zimmer's gone out of business,' says she. Meanwhile, I buy my mother a footbath for her birthday – ninety-two on Wednesday. 'Can I speak to the Manager?' I ask a smart, male assistant, and moan about our phone-call, gruelling journey and the missing walking frame.

This assistant looks rather shifty.

'Are you pretending not to be the Manager?' I ask. He owns up and dredges up a polite look of concern. I suspect it is a pretend one, used day after day on cross daughters and their elderly

255

Michele Hanson

mothers who have fought their way here through crowds and traffic to try wheelchairs, frames and sticks that have disappeared.

Eventually we stagger out. I leave my mother sitting on some boxes of rubbish while I fetch the car. No other form of seating exists. Gone is her dream of the elegant tea at Sagné's. Anyway, it has long since been taken over and inferior gateaux are now served. I return to find her swaying in front of a smart antiques shop window pretending she doesn't need a seat. Better to stand and suffer than to sit and be mistaken for an indigent.

At least she can use the relaxing luxury birthday footbath when she gets home. Wrong again. 'Do not use if your feet are swollen and you have varicose veins.' We are in for a jolly birthday.

Mutton Dressed as Lamb

Rosemary was driving me into town the other morning when she suddenly noticed my leopardskin patterned, clinging top. It was concealed in the main by a large cardigan, but Rosemary could still see the daring neckline.

'What *do* you think you're wearing?' she cried, horrified. 'Please cover it up!'

This was a rather bold garment that the Daughter had encouraged me to buy in last summer's sale. She is mad-keen on this particular shop, which specialises in skimpy, shiny, skin-tight numbers which look like underwear for Jezebels. Her own wardrobe is stuffed with their outfits. Last week she swanned past us in a satiny black number decorated with lace.

'Is that a petticoat she's got on?' shouted my mother. 'I've got one like that.' So naturally I had hesitated before buying the offensive top, but the Daughter was adamant, and as I secretly like clinging, pretend leopardskin, I bought it and wore it brazenly all over the place, until Rosemary's comment.

'What's the matter with it?' I asked. 'Is it mutton dressed as lamb?'

'Even lamb shouldn't go out dressed like that at nine a.m. on a Monday morning,' snapped Rosemary strictly, then she pointed out a smartly dressed woman of our age, striding by in slacks, dark jacket and demure shirt. 'Now I wouldn't mind you looking like that,' she said, but then she spotted the woman's belt, with a huge gold buckle and her pigs'-trotter high heels, and changed her mind.

Apparently, there is a fearfully strict dress code for women of our age to save us from looking foolish. Anything figure-hugging, ostentatious or even mildly erotic is forbidden. After all, what is the benefit of a cleavage that has turned into a pit of wrinkles, or curves that have turned into lumps? Better to be swaddled up to the neck in fabric.

Or is it? Yesterday Olga brought Beverly to tea, our age, with bright pink hair, dazzling purple frock, jewellery glittering away. Olga's clothes were also wildly patterned, but I had my customary mutton-drudge outfit on. I cut a dull figure at table.

'I go for colour and extravagant jewellery,' said Beverly, illuminating the kitchen. 'Aren't we lucky,' said she, 'there's no such thing as a glamorous old man.' I definitely prefer her dress code. Who made the other one anyway? Perhaps I should have bought two of those tops.

Street of Shame

Our street is becoming a scrapyard. The Cable workers have left it littered with mess and now it is filling up with wrecked, stolen cars. Gangs of youths rampage up and down, playing with the rubble and wrecked cars and cheerily running nails along the shiny paintwork of the new ones. Dare I let my mother out on her little daily walk to the corner? We live on the Lower East Side.

Gangs of wild girls and boys sit on the low walls, the street rings with obscenities. Rosemary heard a particularly foul volley of abuse from one loitering youth as she tended her front garden the other day. He was addressing a girl at an upstairs window.

'I don't think you should speak like that in the street,' said Rosemary strictly.

'Sorry Miss,' said the youth, ever so politely, but we suspect he was pretending. I spotted him a few days later bashing a For Sale sign to pieces and strewing it about the street. I told him off, of course, but he only brandished the sign fiercely at my head, roared some even filthier abuse and hurled it into the front garden.

Although I am a liberal and understanding grown-up, this sort of things gets me longing, briefly, for the reintroduction of the stocks. I am keen to have a row of them at each junction, filled with yobs, so that we can lean on our sticks and Zimmers, mocking and throwing things, but as we're all civilised nowadays, we phoned the Council and the police instead, begging them to remove the wrecks, so that our street isn't such an attractive playground for maniacs.

Nothing much seems to have happened. They've been round, had a stare, some more have come, inspected and gone, but the cars remain. Can the police move them? No, the Council must. Can the Council remove these ruined, untaxed vehicles? No, they must do a search first and ask the police.

How odd. They can clamp and remove your normal, functioning motor car in a trice, but these are untouchable. So I ring again and pester. The man who does the search has gone on holiday. No one takes over in his absence. A message will be left for him.

'Would you like the registration numbers?' I ask.

'Might as well,' says the official in a relaxed way.

Another row of stocks please.

Nasty Taste of the Future

My friend Munch has fallen from a ladder while painting the ceiling and broken some ribs. Ouch! She must take ten deep breaths on the hour, each of which feels like a dagger in her heart. But far worse than the murderous pain is the warning of what is to come.

'This is what old age must be like,' cries Munch over the phone. 'You see the dust up there, you know your hair needs washing and you can't do anything about it.' She can't get her knickers or trousers on or off, she can't open screw-tops.

'Suppose I was very old and all alone,' says she poignantly, 'and I couldn't open my jar of marmalade!'

No wonder she is in a blind panic. Being an Occupational Therapist, she has seen the ghastly truth: the institutions and nursing homes, the underpaid and overworked crotchety staff, the miserable little teas, but all very well presented with lovely decor, to impress the punters and their families.

She has visited old ladies in stifling little rooms and found them nodding off, perhaps unaccustomed to central heating, doped by the stuffy heat, their final months or years spent alone and sweltering, no pets allowed. Lying on her back trying to breathe deeply, Munch's imagination is naturally running riot. She sees herself, should she become frail and helpless, wrenched from her airy, pleasant flat with garden and stuffed into a tiny hothouse, her beloved cat disposed of and only a Tamagotchi toy to play with.

I reported this incident to Rosemary, expecting sympathy for Munch, but she only pooh-poohed the whole affair. I should have known she would. She doesn't worry at all about old age and takes such dreadful risks that she probably won't have one. Last week she had a nasty attack of vertigo, lay about helplessly and tottered around as if on board ship. Then, with her head whirling and her leg still not properly recovered from the horrid break, she decided to climb a ladder and put up a new blind.

Naturally I told her off strictly and banned her from ladder-climbing, but she only laughed fiercely. 'Elderly does not mean incapacitated,' she bellowed. Meanwhile, Munch is planning to buy a blunderbuss and fire from her windows at anyone who *comes to take her away*. At least they will both go out with a bang.

Sad Party

My friend Fielding went to a salsa music works party last week, but nobody female spoke to him for longer than twenty seconds. He attributes this to his age – twenty to thirty years older than the other guests. And he foolishly went without his wife.

'They all thought I was there to pick someone up,' whispered Fielding, frightfully embarrassed. Was he? No. But it might have seemed so. He repeated one of his conversation-openers. 'I can't do salsa but I'm very good at jiving.' Women just stared at him with a *who-is-this-person?* kind of look. *'Jiving* brought age into the equation,' droned Fielding, 'and I had to shout because the music was loud.'

Strangely enough he didn't mind the thunderous noise. Although a grown-up, he is still keen on roaring, belting pop music. He has not yet understood that a squillion-decibel throbbing wall of sound can be isolating. One cannot penetrate it with subtlety and wit. His intricate little personality would be blasted to hell by the din and only his outward appearance would be noticed – someone balding and jiving. No wonder young women rejected him.

These new noise levels restrict my outings enormously. I first noticed them at a Who concert in the Seventies. My ears rang with pain for hours afterwards and that was fairy bells compared to nowadays, so I avoid concerts, clubs, dances, cinemas and parties with music. Sometimes I try ear-plugs, or sit in a secluded corner or the lavatory, away from the thundering speakers, but usually I stay at home, in front of the whispering television, or tinkle away at my harpsichord. The magic of this instrument, apart from its heavenly sound, is that it never disturbs the neighbours.

Meanwhile, how brave Fielding is to bang on with these Twentieth-Century outings – screaming, going deaf, being ignored. 'It was a case of invisibility,' said he poignantly, but oddly enough he hadn't felt depressed, just a twinge of existential fear.

'Why am I here?' he asked himself. 'Why did I come?' He came because attractive young women asked him, which he found rather flattering at fifty-three. In the end he decided to cut his losses and caught the last tube home. Then he put on some jiving music and did some Fifties shuffling in his living room. A rather pleasant end to the evening.

Crumbling Away

L ast week my mother had an appointment at the rheuma-
tology clinic because her legs don't work properly any
more. She was desperate to go, even with her ghastly backache. What a vile time we had, stuck in hospital forever while
outside the sun blazed down and the only day of summer passed
by. Inside we waited. And waited and waited, my mother occasionally screaming with pain, me stamping about in a temper.

After two and a half hours of nothing I phoned Rosemary
weeping with fury. She dashed to the hospital at once for a
coffee-break and took charge. 'Stop this at once!' said she, as we
sat out in the sun with our coffees. 'It's like having an infant
beside me. Once you're here, you have to go into a time warp.
That's what I do. Your behaviour is appalling.' My mother's
behaviour was much better than mine. She just waited in the
X-ray department, moaning and growing paler.

But what a good job we went. Her back wasn't strained, it
had crumbled. She has osteoporosis and three vertebrae have
gone for a burton. No wonder she's been screaming for weeks.
And there was I thinking it was only a pulled muscle, bossing
my mother about and thinking her a fusspot. Now I feel like a
Nazi.

'This won't last forever,' said the doctor, and mentioned that
it was a pity she hadn't been given HRT years ago. But years ago
my mother lived on the South Coast, where the elderly live in
their squillions, and when a county is clogged to bursting with

265

crumbling pensioners, it tends not to look to the future, possibly hoping that they haven't a future worth bothering about. Why waste money on HR? So here is my mother, ninety-two, bones crumbling and more of a mess to sort out.

When she'd had her X-ray, her blood tests, the X-ray result and verdict, we could go home at last. Nurses will come daily and give her injections. My mother reached her bedroom ashen after five hours in the hospital, still crippled but in a more relaxed mood. At last everybody appreciates her reason for screaming.

'I don't scream for nothing,' says she grimly. Absolutely. Now where is my nice pot of natural yam progesterone cream? Will it work? I expect I'll find out when I'm ninety-two.

Lest We Forget

This morning I rang Rosemary to ask her for a lift to the garage. She was furious. 'My life is only of concern to you when you want something,' she snapped very strictly indeed. 'Have you forgotten what I said I was doing this afternoon?'

Yes I had. And I'd forgotten what she'd been doing this morning. She had told me her plans yesterday morning, but I'd forgotten by five o'clock, so as we walked the dog I asked to be reminded again, but Rosemary refused to tell me. 'You're not interested in what I do,' said she crossly. 'You only want to self-refer.' But she still omitted to tell me today's arrangements. Now they are hidden under the mists of yesterday and for the life of me I can't fish them out again. 'Please tell,' I nagged Rosemary over the phone, but she wouldn't. 'And you didn't even remember to ask me how my interview went on Monday,' shouted Rosemary, warming to her theme, 'AND I almost made myself late for it dashing to the hospital to rescue you at lunch-time.'

How awful. She is right. But I do have an excuse of sorts. As I can hardly remember my own schedule, how can I hope to remember someone else's who isn't even on the premises. Last week I forgot the dentist and my mother's appointment with the Podiatrist. 'Why Podiatrist?' shouts my mother. 'What's wrong with Chiropodist?' My mother wrote Chiropodist rebelliously in her diary, and I wrote appointments in mine. But then we forgot to look at our diaries.

And I keep forgetting to take my thyroid pills. I have a row of little boxes marked with all the days of the week, but I still forget. At least I know which days I've forgotten. Without these magic pills I may grow obese, lethargic, paranoid, depressed and sterile again. My hair will fall out, my eyes bulge, my skin go pasty and my flesh go to suet, but even with this awful possibility threatening, I still can't remember them. What hope for Rosemary?

When she was in a mellower mood, she would overlook these little lapses and call out 'Senior moment!' in a mocking way. 'Senior half-hour. Ha ha!' That's what the Californians call these episodes. Perhaps she has forgotten.

Still Here

My mother has recovered from her hideous crumbly back illness. What a relief. When someone is ninety-two and every so poorly, it is difficult to imagine that they will ever recover. So while my mother and I have plodded through this ghastly ordeal, we have each been secretly planning funerals and expecting the Reaper to call any minute.

I have gone off for my dog-walkies in the morning leaving my mother asleep. There she was, looking white, deathly and motionless. Was she still with us? Should I wake her and find out? Will she still be here after my walkie? Meanwhile my mother was expecting to leave this earth at about four in the morning. Forty-four was my father's favourite number, and as she often finds herself awake at about that time, she's been hoping he might call for her at about four-forty-four a.m. and escort her to wherever it is that one goes.

'You never go alone,' says she mysteriously. Luckily my mother wasn't going anywhere, except out of bed and down into the sunny garden. After four weeks of hell she has started tottering around again and is even contemplating some more bridge and cooking. But we still live on a knife-edge. This broiling weather is dangerous for the elderly. I heard it on telly. The winter was perilous, now the summer is perilous. My mother must keep out of the sun and drink gallons.

We shunt her around the cooler parts of the house until the evening, when she staggers out for a mini-walk along the pavement. But although things are looking up, she is worrying about her rings again. The first thing I must be sure to do before she is whisked away in the ambulance is to take them off, just in case a passing robber whips them from her hand as it dangles helplessly from some godforsaken hospital trolley.

But what will I do with them once I've saved them? 'You said you didn't like them,' cries my mother in a heart-rending way. But I do. I don't remember saying that. I love the rings. Then what if I lose them? Another huge area of anxiety is looming. Hopefully it can be postponed for some time. Each morning I look into her bedroom. Is she breathing? Yes.

'I'm still here!' croaks my mother, every time.

Holiday Values

On the hottest day of the year my friend Fielding took his teenage daughter shopping for trainers. What a frightful outing. I now realise that one of the wonderful things about growing old is that you no longer have to take your daughter shopping for trainers. And you don't have to take her on holiday.

Soon, laden with new trainers, Fielding will be off on hols with his family. This will be a painful interlude for him. The Daughters are deeply ashamed of his bathing trunks, plimsolls and behaviour. 'I'm not allowed to talk to any member of the public,' he moans poignantly. 'No air-hostess, passport official or other families on the beach. I must just pay out lots of money and stay hidden in the shade. My role essentially is not to be there. I'm an unfortunate presence with a wallet.'

He was allowed, last year, to talk to one man at length about Jimi Hendrix, but he may absolutely not speak to any sun-tanned females. Daughters cannot bear the shame of it. His wife, however, may speak freely to anyone, and does.

Luckily for my friend Olivia, her daughter is off to Majorca with a chum. At first Olivia was thrilled. She read the guidebook eagerly, then chatted to the friend's Mummy about her findings. 'There'll be underground caves, Robert Graves, Majorcan Baroque,' she trilled.

'Oh, they won't be doing any of *that*,' said the other Mummy rather tartly. 'It'll be anything cheap, modern and nasty with bars and boys.' Olivia's heart sank but she twittered on, about beautiful picnics under olive trees in the hills, churches, art, ancient sites and classical music. She couldn't seem to stop herself, but it was hopeless. Daughter and her chum would be staying in a British enclave deprived of beauty and culture. Her grip on the Daughter's holiday activities is weakening.

Now that my daughter is nearly twenty, I have no grip at all, but what a relief. Secretly I suspect Daughter's holiday will be shops, boys, bars, beaches, too much sun, late nights and drink, but I am given edited highlights: the weather, the scenery, the charming company. Sometimes I hear of the odd ear infection or burst of food-poisoning so that I can worry from afar, a reminder of times past, and wish that we were together again.

Wind of Change

'Feel that wind blowing up,' says Rosemary ominously, 'and those leaves are turning yellow!' Suddenly the summer is whizzing to a close and with it the end of an era. Our children are leaving home, both off to university.

Daughter has been rather jittery lately. Yesterday she suddenly stood as if frozen in the hall, her eyes staring. 'I'm going away!' she cried. 'Err!'

I am only half worried because I think she's only half going away – just up the road, a hundred miles or so, a couple of hours by car, a moment by fax or telephone. Luckily Daughter is cheered by the arrival of a sort of university starter pack with a list of requirements – a trousseau for her new home.

'It says I need a toaster, kettle, sandwich-toaster, tin-opener, cheese-grater, cutlery, crockery, duvet, fitted sheets . . .' On and on it goes. Daughter is exhilarated by this mammoth list. It means shopping – her favourite leisure pursuit. 'I've *got* to go to Ikea!' she shouts happily.

Boyfriend has bravely offered to go with her. Does he know the way? 'Yes,' says he, white-faced. 'Up the Archway Road, round the North Circular and into Hell.' But it is just something that has to be done, a distraction from the big event: leaving our house, which has at last perhaps assumed a sort of charm – the dog dribbling at mealtimes, the Grandma tottering about, the larder full of food, the frogs plopping in and out of the pond, the mother in the kitchen – all those familiar things that Daughter may miss dreadfully as she sits alone in her cell-like room in the hall of residence. She must compensate by buying up the whole of Ikea.

Surprisingly Rosemary's son has no list. Perhaps boys are different. Or, mindful of Rosemary's finances, he is bravely keeping it a secret, or he's trying not to think of the future. Meanwhile Rosemary drifts around worrying, longing to prepare, but the Son will not allow it. He doesn't care about possessions, as long as he can take his drum kit. But he'll leave the same space behind.

'What are we going to do?' cries Rosemary. 'No more lifts, no more lending ten-pound notes, no more snack foods, no more hordes of young visitors!' We are nearly crying already. Who would have thought it?

Old Dog

What a fright we had on Sunday morning. The dog wouldn't get up. It had a stomach-ache on Saturday, went to the vet, perked up and then on Sunday seemed to have had it. It didn't wag its tail, it couldn't lift its head. Perhaps it was dehydrated. I spooned water into its chops and wept. I ran about the house blubbing and told my mother the tragic news. She remembered the death of her own beloved Boxer dog forty years ago as if it were yesterday and started to cry.

The dog lay motionless. I spooned in more water and stared out of the open kitchen door into the garden in a desolate way. A squirrel appeared just outside. Suddenly the dog rose from the dead and bolted into the garden. The hated squirrel had revived it.

A false alarm this time but I am on permanent red alert, looking after an elderly dog. I can spot an eye ulcer on day one, recognise a tummy-ache, find the special grasses she likes to eat when nauseous, provide an invalid diet. Sylvia is at it too. Her sixteen-year-old cat is very poorly. It staggers about with its head on one side but it still likes its dinner and sitting in the sun. Sylvia knows it hasn't got long to go. She is pampering it shamelessly with all sorts of treats, wrapping its pills in delicacies. Neither of us can go on holiday in case the cat or dog expires in our absence.

And how will I ever manage without the dog? One day soon it won't be there in the back of the car, or snoozing on the sofa, or barking in the garden, lying in the sun, dribbling at the table or waiting and wiggling when I come home or playing with its squeaky. I plan to rush out and buy two more puppies immediately, probably sisters. Sylvia agrees. At least we'll be busy looking after them instead of crying at home in the empty kitchen.

Friends and advisers are beginning to give me odd looks about all this. 'You must give yourself time to grieve,' they say, looking serious. No I mustn't, thank-you. 'Yes you should,' shouts Rosemary, 'so you can pay some attention to me for a change!' That clinches it. A dog would never behave like that.

Operation

I am just about to have an operation. Possibly a couple of ovaries, tubes, some cysts, polyps and fibroids are to be removed, through keyholes or maybe a larger hole, they can't really tell till they get there, and hopefully the whole lot won't be taken out, but who knows?

Perhaps that one-in-a-million chance will happen and while the surgeon is carefully snipping away at a tiny polyp, his hand may slip one millimetre and it'll be goodbye whole womb and I'll come out weeks later like a tyre without an inner tube. Or worse still, I may never come out at all.

These are my little thoughts in the run-up to the operation, so I've updated my will, divulged certain wishes to trusted chums and made Gardener promise to look after the dog.

'You must talk to the anaesthetist,' says Rosemary strictly. 'Remember what happened to me!'

I don't want to remember that. Rosemary very nearly didn't survive her anaesthetic because she forgot to tell anyone about her sleep apnoea and how her throat tends to close up at night. So she was an exception. Mine is a very mundane operation. People have operations every day. 'Don't be silly,' says everyone, 'anaesthetics are very safe nowadays, you're more likely to die crossing the road, blah blah.'

Meanwhile my mother has gone into anxiety overdrive. If anyone's daughter is going to die under an anaesthetic or be found to have some grisly terminal disease, it will be *hers*, she

277

knows it, then how will she manage at ninety-two and her last days will be spent in misery and drudgery and the Daughter will have no mother. Naturally with these thoughts stewing around in her head she is in a fairly volcanic mood and our house is a minefield.

Luckily I don't die. I'm still here in Elizabeth Garrett Anderson Hospital for women, a small oasis of peace and quiet, soon to be shut down and turned into another hotel. But as I lie here recovering, surrounded by saintly nurses, Daughter and other chums visit daily and news of fierce squabbles and tension at home filters through. My mother is Chief of Staff and not everyone is doing as they are told. And she is still on red alert awaiting the Return of the Invalid. And I thought the dangerous bit was over.

Look Back In Horror

For weeks Rosemary has been looking forward to her outing to *Oklahoma*, the stage version. She plans to drag other members of her family and friends along too. I can't imagine why. For me, hell is a musical and I have warned Rosemary repeatedly not to go. She has refused to discuss it. Every time I've queried her judgement, she's just started to sing loudly.

'Oo Oh-Oklahoma where the . . .' she roared as we walked round the block. 'And the farmer and the cowhand shall be friends,' she bellowed in the kitchen and at last she went to see the wretched thing.

Next morning she looked rather grim. 'It was ghastly,' said she, bravely admitting her mistake, but she admired the cast. 'They never stopped kicking their legs in the air and spinning about in pinnies and stockings. Poor things, and they'd already done it once in the afternoon. They must have been absolutely worn out.'

Rosemary's son couldn't quite make it out – a strange entertainment from the past. 'Is there a story?' he asked. 'Is it Music Hall?'

'And how much did all this cost you?' I ask.

'SHUT UP,' shouts Rosemary. She has squandered a fortune. But she felt impelled to go. It was just one of those things she remembered fondly from her youth, like *Milly-Molly-Mandy* and *Anne of Green Gables*. 'And then there was something

279

momentous, something magical when you came across it as a teenage girl.'

What slop! I preferred Rosemary Sutcliffe and all those fierce, rather butch stories of Roman legions and slave galleys, or *White Fang* and Barbara Woodhouse and breathing down horses' noses, then luckily for me, along came Elvis. Shockingly, Rosemary never liked Elvis. 'He was rather too uninhibited,' said she strictly. Had we met at school, we would never have been friends.

But at least this outing has cured Rosemary of nostalgia. She tottered out of the theatre saying briskly, 'That's IT!' It hadn't recreated the feeling of things past, only bored Rosemary to death.

'Serves her right,' I said to Sylvia on our walk, but she sided with Rosemary. '*Oklahoma* was revolutionary!' she cried. 'We'd never had such athletic dancing.' When she was a teenager all she'd had to go wild about was Ivor Novello. Now we have rap, grunge, Lloyd Webber and knickers off at Manumission. Nostalgia will never be what it used to be.

Year of the Penis

I notice that people are bandying the word 'penis' about like never before and it isn't my favourite word. It sounds like something long, thin and pointy like a pencil, which isn't exactly what one is looking for, and that long *ee* makes it sound even thinner. 'Isn't that funny?' I said to Rosemary, 'whereas vagina has an open sound.'

'Stop it!' she shouted. 'You're entering a whole arena that I want nothing to do with.' And who can blame her. Contemplating male genitalia isn't everyone's cup of tea, but we must all do it, because this seems to be the Year of the Penis, what with the President waving his about, Viagra all over the place and the telly schedules stuffed with sex programmes.

Last week one could watch penises on telly for hours on end: pretend ones, real ones, inside and out, stuck with needles, measured, pumped up, simulated and ready to go, or resting. 'Bloody disgraceful,' shouted my mother from her bedroom. Even with her sensitivities blunted by years of Kilroy, Vanessa and Gerry Springer, she was still shocked by the multitude of penises televised this week and the bold investigations into bodies, sex and odd behaviour: ladies with whips and bosoms pumped up almost to bursting, men crawling around swathed in rubber, bare people standing about, doctors and scientists measuring, testing and explaining *and* Monica's saucy reports.

On the positive side, flashers will rather lose their edge. We'll be so used to *those things* that they might as well brandish

281

a corn-on-the-cob. And this tidal wave of information might even act as a nationwide blanket contraceptive. Sexual overload and fatigue will set in. Years ago I saw an artistic Japanese film, *In the Realm of the Senses*, in which the protagonists were at it like knives for ages, until she chopped his penis off, although she adored it. Perhaps she was exhausted. We certainly were. Even though I removed my glasses, I still remember an endless blur of red and purple that made me feel quite ill.

Yesterday, for a change, Sylvia and I took the dogs for a walkie in the fresh air, but our heads were still swimming with penis thoughts from the week's telly. We climbed Kite Hill and gazed down at the London skyline, but it is now marred by large sticky-up buildings. Is there no escape?

Daughter Leaves Home

Last week I drove the Daughter to university. Her trousseau had grown enormous and much of Sainsbury's, Ryman's and Ilkea were stuffed into the car. Daughter had been terrifically calm and well organised, the sun shone, we drove off as if on holiday, but just thirty miles from our destination, someone seemed to have emptied a cutlery drawer into the engine.

The steering wheel juddered, the gears whined, the car's innards clattered away. We vowed to buy a new car. We would get this one mended and *get rid of it*, we promised, please God, if we could just reach the halls of residence with this huge cargo of Daughter's possessions.

We made it, but it was hideous for the Daughter, at the very start of her university life and longing to appear normal, to arrive in a rattling tin can with a pale and sweating mother. And I had been looking forward to this last day with my child, unpacking and crying together. Instead I was towed off by the AA to a hidden garage miles away in the outback, leaving her to unpack all alone.

Mechanics looked at the car in a bleak way. 'Six hundred and fifty if you're lucky,' they droned, 'possibly a thousand.' And my car is only worth sixpence anyway. Then back to the Daughter's lodgings in a taxi. She had unpacked, her room was immaculate, themed blue and silver, and she was partying in the kitchen. We only had time for a quick farewell dinner in

283

the nearest café before I caught the last train home to London, where my mother was waiting in a panic.

What for? I am a grown-up, and from today, so is the Daughter. But my mother was right to be frightened half to death. There was a madman in my train. And the train seemed to be a pre-war model, no buffet, left late and dawdled into town while the maniac hurled himself about from one side of the carriage to the other, banging his head against the windows and screaming 'Nottingham!' in terrible despair. In between screams he glared about in a vicious way, wondering who to attack. I knew it would be me.

Luckily it wasn't. I reached home, fell asleep exhausted and woke in the morning to an empty life. No Daughter. And not even a car to cry in.

Hot Air

Apparently the tea-dances in eighteenth-century Bath were not as delightful as they're cracked up to be. When the assembled company rose en masse to rush to the tea-table, the stench caused one contemporary observer to fall down in a dead faint. He referred to the dancers as so many 'rotting human bellows'.

This description fits me to a tee now that I am on the way downhill. I suspect many of the tea-dancers were mature persons whose innards were beginning to play them up. As one gets older, this sort of problem seems to get worse. The stomach bloats and blocks up and one wanders around like a barrage balloon, unable to bend in the middle, so sitting at table, in restaurants, theatres and cinemas becomes something of an ordeal. At least this is my personal experience. I tend to stay at home, where I can lie flat on the floor when necessary.

But flicking through a health cookery book, I notice a cure for bloated abdomens filled with putrefaction and blocked gases. Our prayers are answered! I throw away the chip pan and whack my mother on to a health diet of fennel á la gréque, tabouleh with mint and parsley, organic potatoes and a little delicately grilled fish. Soon it will all be gliding through her happy bowels, unimpeded.

She is furious and stabs at her plate. 'These aren't cooked, this has no bloody taste and this stinks,' she cries. 'It's all going down the lavatory!' Just wait. Tomorrow she'll be force-fed globe artichokes, cabbage and plums for irritability and anger.

My friend Fielding is also opposed to health food. The staff in his local health shop are no incentive. 'One's a mountain, one's a matchstick and the other talks rubbish,' he shouts offensively, still smarting from the forty-eight-hour fruit diet his wife ordered to stop him turning to suet. For two days he shivered and lived mainly in the lavatory and then collapsed with flu, but only gained more weight, because he had sneaked downstairs at midnight and eaten whole pounds of cheese.

Now my builder tells me of his mate's diet. Nothing for breakfast, an apple for lunch, then half a pound of butter on his potatoes at supper, plus three avocados and a bed-time snack the size of your average person's daily intake.

Fortunately, tea-dances have faded out.

Bottom-Wiper

We arrive at the Heath in the car. The dog and I leap out and leave Rosemary to lock her side, but I hear that the door hasn't shut correctly. 'Is it locked properly?' I ask. Rosemary is incensed. 'How dare you?' she roars. 'I have locked this door hundreds of times, I am perfectly capable of doing it, and you are a BOTTOM WIPER!'

What will the public out for their Saturday walks think? Will they realise that this is a metaphor? 'You are always doing this!' Rosemary rants on. 'You don't trust anyone to do anything properly, you're always checking up!'

She doesn't understand that it's anxiety, not mistrust. How can I be sure that she'll turn my oven off when I'm out, call in on my mother, save me Sunday's paper, draw my blinds when I'm away? In her place I would forget. I did yesterday.

I was meant to defrost Rosemary's casserole in my microwave, but I forgot to check and defrost longer. Twenty minutes later, her guests eagerly awaiting their dinner, Rosemary rang again. She should have rung much earlier to check. I wouldn't have minded, because I'm used to anxious and fastidious bottom-wipers. My mother is one.

Rosemary's mummy probably let her get on with things, but my mummy worried over and supervised clean bottoms for longer than average. She still does, metaphorically of course. 'Have you turned the oven off?' she calls. 'Have you locked the door/put the chicken in the fridge/turned the bath

287

off/phoned the bank/put salt on the fish/found the bridge table?'

'Yes, yes, yes, yes, yes, yes, yes.'

'Are you sure?/Have you checked?/How much?/When?/Show me.'

'Yes, yes, yes, yes, all right.'

And then, perhaps overwhelmed and confused by the spray of bullet questions, I may forget something, so my mother's anxiety is reinforced and she checks and questions all the more. So imagine my surprise at Rosemary's outburst over my one weedy little question. It reminded her of all my other little questions over the years and she is furious.

This is a wonderful thing about a dog, especially for a metaphorical bottom-wiper. I can't say it often enough. You can supervise it and check and look after its physical needs for ever and ever amen until it is quite grown-up and nobody minds. And if absolutely necessary, you can even wipe its bottom.

Sick Children

Daughter arrives home for the weekend from university with a hacking, foghorn cough. My mother staggers downstairs to make stews to stoke up the beloved Grandchild. She must be refuelled with huge dinners and snacks, lemon and honey and cosseting before returning to her relatively wild, gruelling and undernourished life as a student.

All through the weekend we toil away, feeding, pandering, revitalising and strengthening the Daughter. At last her health is on the mend. Then just prior to departure she rings a chum up there and hears a bit of news.

'Two people have got meningitis!' she cries cheerily, and rushes upstairs to pack. Luckily my mother, the Anxiety Queen, doesn't hear this, but I am sick with fright. Off goes the Daughter, possibly debilitated by her cough and weakened lungs, to Plague City. Any germ or virus hanging around up there is bound to home in on *my* child. Then what? Will her symptoms be recognised? Will she reach hospital in time? Who will look after my Mother and Dog while I'm up there at her bedside in hospital?

I spend a more or less sleepless night waking repeatedly in a boiling sweat and dreaming of death and disease. I am on the blower to the university at first light to enquire about the epidemic, incognito because Daughter will be browned off if she finds that her pesky mother is still flapping about after her, even though she is now a grown-up.

But what a good job that I phoned. There is no epidemic and no meningitis. Only one suspected case which proved to be a false alarm, *and* the Meningitis Awareness Van has been round. I can breathe properly again.

Meanwhile I do a quick neighbourhood survey. My child is only one of many. Rosemary's boy is also ill in his lonely room, stoically brewing up packets of chicken soup, and sucking Zubes, then tottering to lectures. Olivia's boy is struggling with tonsillitis, Mrs X's son has given up and come home, legs shaking, weak and dizzy, for an extended pit-stop and overhaul before he plunges back into the stew of infection.

I ring Daughter for a progress report. 'My friends are here,' says she cheerily. 'They've all caught it now. Listen!' I hear multiple coughs in the background. 'They're looking after me.' Oh good. Now I can really relax.

Cataract Queue

M y mother is on the cataract waiting list. As it's meant to be six months long and she's been waiting seven, perhaps she'll be nearing the top. I ring to find out.

'You mother is not an urgent case,' says the List-Organiser. 'She's routine.' Well of course. My mother's ninety-two, completely blind in one eye, can only read huge print, must sit two inches from the telly, keeps bumping into things and can't find her false teeth. She is to spend the remainder of her time on earth tottering about in a mist.

But we are in luck. As she has osteoporosis and has just recovered from a crumbling broken back, it is imperative that she doesn't bump into things and fall over. The Back Specialist writes to the Eye Specialist to see if she can be made a priority. He dictates this letter as we watch. Bliss. Things are on the move.

Eight days pass. I ring the Eye Department. They have heard nothing from the Back Specialist. My mother is still mouldering at the bottom of the list. Why? Oh, it takes two weeks for a letter to arrive, be seen, shown to the Specialist and a decision to be made. But the letter hasn't even arrived yet. And anyway, the waiting list isn't six months, it's a year.

With any luck, if you put a ninety-two-year-old woman on a year-long waiting list, she'll drop dead before she gets to the top, saving the NHS time and money. Meanwhile, where is the Back Specialist's letter?

No one has seen it. My mother's file is not in the normal place. A search is carried out, the file found, the letter discovered. It will be typed out at once and faxed to the Eye Consultant. Poor Secretary has three Consultants' work to do and hasn't had time to do it yet. Now we're short of midwives, nurses *and* medical secretaries. Next day I track the fax down. It has gone to another secretary who kindly whacks it into the Eye Consultant's tray with our request underlined in red.

But Consultant is away until next week. Then she may decide whether my mother, one among hundreds of fading, semi-blind elderly patients, should become a priority. And we live in the First World.

This operation costs £2–3,000 privately. Apparently Marxism is making a comeback. Not a moment too soon.

Hallowe'en

This year I forgot Hallowe'en. I no longer have a young
child to remind me of it. I only remembered at six p.m.,
too late to buy tons of little sweets for the dreaded Trick-or-
Treaters.

Good. I hate Trick-or-Treat. Not only does it encourage
extortion and greed, terrify pensioners, upset the dog and rot
everyone's teeth, but it also brings back painful memories of
past Hallowe'ens spent trudging round the streets with the
Daughter and her little flock of chums in their ghost and witch
outfits, hovering on the dark and chilly pavements while they
rushed up and down garden paths begging, driving the neighbours mad and fighting over their spoils.

And I always *had* to go drizzling along behind them because
I knew that the city streets were thick with psychopaths and
molesters just waiting to snatch children away. What bliss that
I never have to do it again. This time I turned off all the lights
and rejoiced in the dark. Then the Trick-or-Treaters would
think we were out. I was Scrooge over a candle in a back room,
so not a chink of light could give me away.

But today's children are very bold. They braved the darkness
and knocked. The dog hurled itself at the front door, barking
like a fiend. From her bedroom my mother croaked loudly, 'Go
away!' She was thrilled with her role. The rain bucketed down,
waves of nastiness poured from our home and soon the little
Trick-or-Treaters ran away . . . to Rosemary's house, with its

welcoming pumpkin lantern. *And* she had stocked up with sweeties. She felt kind and mellow all week.

But she too has her bitter memories – of Fireworks Day: the huge expense, stiff necks and exhausted Mummies busy making hot drinks and sausages while the Husbands play outdoors with bonfires.

Then one particular year, a neighbour invited us to their communal bonfire. We were all to bring fireworks and food. Only one house would be in turmoil instead of a whole streetful. We arrived rosy-cheeked with excitement.

'Five pounds each please,' said the Host. Rosemary felt rather let down. This was meant to be a community effort, not a business opportunity. And coming hot on the heels of Hallowe'en, another gruelling festivity is not what one wants. Luckily, at our age, we don't have to have any of it.

Hard Lessons

L ast year Rosemary left Higher Education. She was made redundant. But what luck that she got out when she did. According to my friend Mr X, Higher Education is going down the drain. Mr X teaches in an art college where there are too many students, too few staff and Management on a distant planet. Naturally everyone was griping, so to sort out their problems, Management paid NOP vast sums for a survey to find out what was going on down there among the staff.

Management read the survey and produced a booklet in response (more thousands of pounds), which recommended the staff should *live our image*, managers should *walk the job* and *a specialist consultant* should be employed to *recommend the most appropriate methods of face-to-face communications*.

'Why didn't they just ask me?' shouted Mr X, stamping round his studio and waving the *paper-based information* about. 'I'd have told them. More staff, more money and less bullshit!' But he can't get near them. Management are often elusive young creatures who avoid staff dining- and common-rooms and are often abroad for weeks on end searching the globe for rich foreign students, who may not have adequate skills for college courses, but at least they have adequate money.

Meanwhile Rosemary's old college recently offered her some part-time work. It was really her old job back disguised as sessional teaching, for a quarter of her original pay. She turned them down. She has another job now, where people speak normal English. She doesn't have to worry about *learning out-comes*, *personal induction development*, *target participants*, or *conventional badges of fitness*. But sadly, she felt she may have been discarded because of her age. Old means experienced, which means expensive, but Management-speak is the perfect way to get rid of the elderly. Faced with a wall of incomprehensible verbal crap, they may blame themselves or Alzheimer's and retire in despair.

But Mr X is hanging on and learning to cope. It isn't easy. He must grade without marking, spread himself thinly among the hordes of students and try not to punch Management. To keep himself from going completely raving mad, he collects the new phrases.

'I've got some more,' he yelled over the phone yesterday. '*Generic models of description and delivery. Triangulate the audit. Increased student awareness of ethics clarity.* Beat those!'

Any suggestions?

Queen of Tact

Olga came round in one of her favourite jumpers which she'd found in an Oxfam shop. It was brightly coloured, decades old, hand-knitted and the wool slightly matted with age, but Olga loved it and as she is an artist, she knew it was beautiful.

My mother was horrified. She rummaged desperately in her cupboards and hauled out all her old jumpers, fluffy mohair and knitted by herself, and begged Olga to take one. 'It's better than that thing,' she said in her forthright way, pointing at Olga's beloved woolly. Luckily Olga was very keen on my mother's offering. She is to have it shortly for her birthday.

'I wouldn't wipe the floor with the one *she* was wearing,' said my mother later. Perhaps she is learning tact. She kept this final damning critique until after Olga had left. This was no mean feat for my mother. She usually sees tact as an untruth. If someone looks a fright, then she *must* tell them. 'But suppose they don't want to know?' I ask. Tough. My mother cannot lie.

'You've got a fat bum,' she called out last week, seeing me outlined in a long pink vest.

'It's the pink,' I shouted, ripped it off and put on a black one. But then I foolishly wore some baggy trousers.

'Your bum is definitely getting fatter,' cried my mother again, and then she advised me to buy a wig. She is on a roll. Spotting Rosemary and me trudging off for our dog-walk she felt a need to blurt out the truth again.

'You both look schlumperdich!' she called. I translated for Rosemary. Drudgy. This is nothing new. My mother has often nagged Rosemary. 'Why d'you wear those dark colours?' she has moaned on. 'They do nothing for your complexion. You need a bit of colour!' Rosemary doesn't even own a lipstick. My mother can scarcely move without one.

Last night Rosemary and I sat in her living room looking plain. 'I'm not attractive,' said Rosemary in a heart-rending way.

'You are!' I shouted, *and* Rosemary is saintly. After all this she *still* admires my mother. 'She's marvellous. So smart. She must have looked stunning in her youth,' says Rosemary like a disciple. She paused for a moment. 'Will you buy me a lipstick for Christmas?'

Can my mother's harsh strategy be working?

Bye Bye Baby

Daughter came home again for the weekend from university. 'I'm going home on Monday morning,' says she blithely. *Home?* What a blow to me. Her home is now elsewhere. On Monday she packs her own bag, makes her own Marmite and cucumber sandwiches for the train and doesn't even ask for a lift to the station.

How marvellous! At last Daughter is a grown-up – independent, able to travel about Britain by herself and no longer needs her packing and homework supervised. I have been looking forward to this for years. Recently I have even ordered her not to ask me for lifts. 'I'm working!' I have shouted crabbily. 'It may not look like it to you but I am working, I too have another life and I am not your chauffeur and chambermaid blah blah . . .'

But just as Daughter leaves the house, I lift up her bag. It weighs a ton. And she hasn't really left herself much time, so she'll have to rush up and down stairs and escalators lugging the enormous bag, then she'll be all hot, exhausted and upset and may miss her train *and* be late for her lecture.

Suddenly I have a desperate longing to drive her to the station. I bite my lip and wave daughter off. She staggers off down the road. Will she pull a muscle in her arm? Will she wreck her spine? I address myself strictly. 'Do not offer her a lift to Euston. Your baby is a grown-up.' I am in turmoil in the kitchen. An hour passes. Will Daughter ring sobbing from the station because she's missed the train? No. Everything must be fine. *I am not needed.*

Luckily Daughter has left a chum staying in her room here temporarily while he searches for a flat. Good. I can wake him up in the mornings when he oversleeps and sometimes cook his dinner. And his mates visit and tramp up and down the stairs. The house is still full of youth. Daughter whizzes home at weekends to visit them, but soon the chum's leaving as well. Then my house will be as empty as Rosemary's.

Rosemary's boy is further away and even more independent. He rarely phones and demands little, so she's sent him an Advent calendar. 'It's a grown-up one,' says she sensibly, 'without chocolates of course.'

Glad Tidings

A t last Rosemary is to spend Xmas in London. She can't afford to go to her luxury cottage in Cornwall and is stuck here with us. We'd like to combine and have Xmas together but will our families agree?

My mother is not too keen. She has shared Xmas lunch once before and it was ruined because *the other people* overcooked the sprouts and we all had to behave properly at the table and pull crackers instead of collapsing halfway through dinner on to the sofa in a slobby way.

Daughter, however, is keen on a shared Xmas. Her view of the festive period is not as sour as my mother's. She feels that an influx of cheery neighbours will diffuse tension and dullness in our house, like a sparkly tributary bringing freshness and life to the turgid waters of the main river.

'We need Christians for a proper Christmas,' says she strictly and Rosemary's family fit the bill.

But will they want to come? So far, they are split 50–50. Rosemary and one daughter say yes, but the son and other daughter are not so sure. And who can blame them? Xmas is often tempestuous in our house. People stamp off into their rooms in a temper, or won't finish dinner, or don't like their presents, or don't say thank-you in quite the right way, or the dog eats too many turkey snacks and vomits. Or we all run sobbing to the houses of various friends and neighbours, wondering how they manage to be nice to each other.

Rosemary does have reservations. She's had one meal in our house and had to leave before pudding. 'You don't lay the table properly,' said she. 'You don't stay sitting down, any of you. I was waiting for a fork and I realised it would never come.'

But hopefully this year will be different. All we have to do is convince the doubters that our plan is a winner. We don't mind catering for everyone. Vegetarian option will be provided, the table will be beautifully set, I promise.

'I make very good brandy-butter,' says Rosemary, 'and my Baby Boy wants prawn cocktail for starters, and then we can play charades!'

Perhaps it isn't such a good idea after all.

Eyeballs

It's all eyeballs in our house. The dog's eyeball has festered for months and now my mother has finally had her cataract operation. With a local anaesthetic. Ow. She saw it coming. And her ward was plastered with technicolour eyeball pictures.

It has been a difficult time for me because I'm not keen on eyeballs. The thought of anything happening to an eyeball makes me break out into a boiling sweat, except for my legs, which go icy-cold and shrink. In this condition I must put my mother's eye-drops in four times a day. To help things along I have a shout just before the drops. Aaaargh! Naturally my mother is hurt.

'You don't mind the dog's eyeball,' she says poignantly. 'What's so terrible about mine?' But the dog's eyeball is plain brown and looks rather more robust. My mother's looks delicate and more like a bare eyeball.

And it isn't only eyeballs. As the years pass by I am growing more and more vapourish. Any glimpse of physical injury will do it – any blood on the telly, any suggestion of knives or razors and I'm sweating and fainting again. Any births, deaths, wars, catastrophes or unfortunate animals and I'm blubbing away. To avoid mockery, I watch Pet Rescue alone in my bedroom where I can cry undisturbed.

'It's your menopause,' says Rosemary strictly. 'It's a transitional phase. You'll be better soon.' But she's wrong. Phases don't last for twenty-five years. I ring my friend Fielding for a change of topic, but bad luck. He has just been to the eye hospital to have two styes-turned-cysts removed.

'It was the Duke of Gloucester Ward!' he shouts, and describes the operation, which he remembers in detail, thanks to local anaesthetic. His eyelids were stuck with daggers and knives, then he was sent home, bandaged and bleeding, in a taxi. Taxi driver had to lead him to his garden gate and open his front door for him and his daughter won't come home because he looks such a fright. She is staying elsewhere. Feeling rather hurt, Fielding sank onto the sofa and turned the telly on for some football, but his eyes were veiled in blood and bandages and he couldn't watch it, which has wrecked his holidays. But at least my mother can now thread a needle without her glasses on. Happy Xmas.

Turkey Halves

Rosemary and I never did get to spend Xmas together. We had one divine morning on the sunny Heath with the dog planning it, then things went suddenly and horribly wrong. First Rosemary lost her car keys somewhere in the grass and we couldn't get home. Daughter had to be called to fetch us and my family turned against Rosemary, for losing keys and borrowing our table.

Actually, Rosemary had done nothing wrong, but this was the pre-Xmas period when people are brewing up for festive tempers and she just happened to be in the way. So she chickened out of the shared Xmas. And she wasn't the only one to panic. Concerned neighbours, hearing of our plan, invited Rosemary's son to Xmas lunch with them, to save him from hell.

But by now Rosemary had already ordered our turkey. What were we to do? There was only one solution. Cut the turkey in half. I ran round to tell the butcher. He had known of the risks but was hoping for the best.

'Yes or no?' asked Butcher anxiously.

No. Butcher had to chop the turkey in two. 'It'll be fine,' said he looking worried, and wrapped the halves up neatly. 'Just keep basting it,' he cried rather poignantly. 'Happy Christmas!'

If only. The Daughter adores Xmas and had been busy for weeks, decorating, arranging twinkly lights and pretty cards, sprinkling cranberries about, shopping, shopping and shopping.

But my mother loathes the whole performance. She is still waiting for the Messiah to come.

'Happy Christmas!' cried the Daughter cheerily on Xmas morning.

'I wish I'd died in the night,' groaned my mother, setting the tone for the day, then she staggered to the kitchen to make chestnut stuffing. Daughter and I battled on with the cooking, extra basting, presents, lighting fires, being cheery, but there was no escaping our tradition of an Xmas-day scream. It happened just before lunch, for no specific reason. It was just that all the year's aggravation had been simmering away to erupt like Monserrat and foul up the festivities. Rosemary had a lucky escape. But we pressed on, our half turkey was heavenly, we all wore our presents, visited neighbours for tea, things calmed down, Rosemary and I are still friends and the dog wasn't even sick. A triumph by our standards.